EQUAL HOUSING
OPPORTUNITY

The California Fair Housing Encyclopedia

A guide to fair housing practices for owners and managers of residential rental property in California

LAW OFFICES OF **Kimball, Tirey & St. John LLP**

7676 Hazard Center Drive, Suite 900-A
San Diego, CA 92108
800-338-6039
www.kts-law.com

Prepared by the
Kimball, Tirey and St. John LLP
Fair Housing Practice Group

ISBN: 0-9729019-1-4

2018 Edition, First Printing
Printed in the United States of America

The California Fair Housing Encyclopedia

Limits of Liability and Disclaimer of Warranty

Kimball, Tirey & St. John LLP have used their best efforts in the preparation of this
Encyclopedia. These efforts include the development, research and verification of
all information herein contained. No warranty of any kind, expressed or implied, is
made with regard to the information. Making copies of this book, or any portion
thereof, for any purpose other than your own non-commercial use, without permission is a violation of United States copyright law. Previous editions of this Encyclopedia do not provide the most current legal information on Federal and California Fair Housing Law.

*The information is general in nature and is not intended as legal advice.
Readers should always consult with a knowledgeable fair housing attorney
to discuss the facts of their particular situation.*

Kimball, Tirey & St. John LLP shall not be liable in the event of incidental or conse-
quential damages in connection with or arising out of the use of any information
herein contained.

> *Caution: The laws change regularly, and while they are current in
> this Encyclopedia as of January 1, 2018, they are subject to change
> at any time without notice. Court decisions and governmental guid-
> ance memoranda may also have legal impact.*

Table of Contents

Stay up to date! It's time to toss the 2017 edition of the Encyclopedia.

This Encyclopedia is designed to be easily read and understood by owners and managers of residential rental property in California. Although much of it is applicable to any property in the U.S., the emphasis in this Encyclopedia is on property located within California. It provides an overview of the most common fair housing situations encountered in rental housing. Consider it both as an educational tool and a reference for fair housing issues and questions that arise on your property.

Reminder: Fair housing situations can be extremely complicated and always have their own unique set of facts.
Therefore, do not consider the information contained in this Encyclopedia as legal advice for your specific situation.
It is general information that can help you in your day-to-day management practices.

Fair housing training can reduce your risk of discrimination claims. If a situation arises, however, we want to talk to you *early* in the process while there is still time to avoid a formal complaint. Sometimes there may be no clear guidance in an unusual case—no specific language in the law or known administrative interpretations and no relevant court decisions that apply. That's when it is critical to draw on the experience of your fair housing advisors.

If you suspect you may have a potential fair housing situation or find yourself in the middle of one, immediately contact an attorney who specializes in fair housing, such as those in the Fair Housing Practice Group at Kimball, Tirey & St. John LLP. If the damage has already been done, we can attempt to find the least painful resolution.

This Encyclopedia is designed *to complement* your annual fair housing trainings—*not to replace* training. You can never learn too much about fair housing. Make it a point to learn as much as you can, to attend live or on-line trainings every chance you get and to establish a fair housing library of current reference information.

Note: There is some brief repetition in a few of the articles because each section in this guide is designed to stand alone—as it does in an encyclopedia. ◆

ADA (Americans with Disabilities Act)

In July of 1990, Congress passed the Americans with Disabilities Act (ADA), which provided a number of protections for persons with disabilities in the areas of public accommodations and employment. It became effective in 1991. California followed suit, adopting the ADA and making it part of the California Unruh Civil Rights Act. In fact, every violation of the ADA in this state is an automatic violation of the Unruh Act.

The federal ADA was amended in 2010. This amendment contains new physical accessibility requirements. However, if a property was in compliance with the 1991 ADA standards at the time of the amendment, it doesn't have to be brought up to the 2010 standards until it is added to or remodeled (Keep in mind that some activities, such as resurfacing your parking lot, will likely require you to update your parking area to the then current codes).

On the other hand, if a property was not previously brought up to the 1991 standards, then the property must be modified to comply with the 2010 standards.

> Warning: We recommend you have a CASp (Certified Accessibility Specialist), with specific knowledge of ADA and California accessibility requirements, conduct a physical evaluation of your property to determine its vulnerability for becoming a target of an ADA lawsuit.

Don't confuse the ADA with the Fair Housing Act requirements. Although there are some overlaps and some of the definitions of disability may be interchangeable, they are very different in their substance and application.

Key difference
- Title III of the ADA pertains to the **public areas** of your property.
- Fair housing law pertains to all the rest of it, primarily the **private areas** of your property and also the common areas.

Public areas of the property
Under the ADA, all areas of a property to which the public is invited must be accessible by persons with disabilities. (This law does not pertain to areas such as individual apartments, laundry rooms and fitness centers that are used *only* by your residents and their guests.)

- Parking provided for prospective lessees and your rental office is the primary public areas on your property. "Accessibility" is generally considered to mean "wheelchair accessible" (although there are specific requirements for the vision and hearing impaired as well). A person who uses a wheelchair should be able to get from the parking area to your office to do business. If the person can't, it is going to be very difficult to defend an ADA complaint.

- Even if your rental office is located in the *manager's apartment*, the portions used for business also fall under ADA guidelines. A potential applicant must be able to get to and into the apartment office.

- Your model apartments should also be accessible since they are marketing tools for the public and may be governed by the California Unruh Act. If there is no way to make a model accessible, you should find other means of demonstrating its features, such as through a video, virtual tour, brochure or display. An example of an inaccessible model would be when, in a three-story walk-up, the third floor units are the only ones with vaulted ceilings and fireplaces and one of them is a model.

- If you rent out your recreation areas or community room to outsiders, or if you hold neighborhood swim meets in your pool area, or if you allow the property to be used for a public purpose such as for a polling place during an election, those areas will be considered to be "public areas" and should, therefore, also be accessible. This includes parking and paths to those areas. If only residents and guests use the facilities and amenities, the ADA does not apply (although fair housing laws may apply in certain circumstances).

If your property was built <u>before</u> 1990
Properties built before 1990 are required to comply with the ADA. No one is completely "grandfathered in;" otherwise only new properties would have public areas that are accessible. This means that all properties are required to remove the existing barriers to accessibility.

Exceptions: You are not required to make a change <u>if it would not be considered "readily achievable and technically feasible" under the circumstances</u>. "Readily achievable" means easily accomplishable and able to be carried out without much difficulty or expense. The standard for determining what is readily achievable is complicated and includes the following analysis:

1. The nature and cost of the action;
2. The overall financial resources of the site or sites involved; the number of persons employed at the site; the effect on expenses and re sources; legitimate safety requirements necessary for safe operation, including crime prevention measures; or any other impact of the action on the operation of the site;
3. The geographic separateness, and the administrative or fiscal relationship, of the site or sites in question to any parent corporation or entity;
4. If applicable, the overall financial resources of any parent corporation or entity; the overall size of the parent corporation or entity with respect to the number of its employees; the number, type, and location of its facilities; and
5. If applicable, the type of operation or operations of any parent corporation or entity, including the composition, structure, and functions of the workforce of the parent corporation or entity.

As you can see, what is "readily achievable" will have to be determined on a case-by-case basis in light of the nature and cost of the barrier removal and the resources available. For example, the owner of an eight-unit building might not be expected to make a costly modification that might be a less significant expenditure for a larger property. Some properties may be built on hillsides or have other configurations that may make them difficult, extremely expensive or even impossible to modify.

Accessibility Plan: If your property is not already in full compliance, it is essential to have an accessibility plan in place that is being implemented on a regular basis.

- The plan should identify what barriers exist, what is being done or has been done to remove them, timelines, costs, etc.
- If there are justifiable reasons why you cannot remove a particular barrier, be sure to have documentation supporting your reasons.
- If there are any delays in the implementation, be sure there are documented reasons for them as well.

Properties built <u>after</u> 1990
Properties constructed after 1990 must comply with the ADA. Additionally, properties with first occupancy after March 13, 1991, should have been built

in compliance with the Federal Fair Housing Act's construction accessibility requirements.

If a property is not in compliance with either or both laws, owners may face costly retrofitting and other fines and penalties. In fact, other properties built by the same company throughout the country may also be investigated for compliance. Retrofits alone can cost many millions of dollars, not to mention the possible imposition of punitive damages. Under Title III, the Department of Justice can obtain civil penalties of up to $55,000 for a first violation and up to $110,000 for subsequent ADA violations.

In recent years, virtually hundreds of newly-constructed properties throughout the U.S. have been targeted for non-compliance with both the ADA and the Fair Housing Act. It is one of the most common disability complaints. How does this happen? There appears to be plenty of blame to go around for this predicament; consequently, a variety of defendants have been sued, from the developers and contractors to the architects, engineers and building owners. In the past, building inspectors have not been required to monitor accessibility requirements, so the building may be completed before the violations are uncovered. Frequent audits before and during construction by a certified expert can be extremely useful.

Typical accessibility modifications

Imagine you are an applicant in a wheelchair, or that you have invited a person with a disability to accompany you in your apartment search. Picture yourself arriving at *your own* rental office. What barriers would you encounter?

If there is a public (future resident) parking area for the rental office, is there at least one marked handicapped parking space (with the blue lines)? If only one space is provided, it should be van-accessible or 96 inches wide with a 60-inch aisle and the appropriate signage. You need at least one accessible space if you have *up to* 25 parking spaces for the public. There are requirements for additional spaces if you are fortunate enough to have more than 25 public parking spaces.

- *Curbs:* Can you get up the curb to the sidewalk? Is a ramp or curb-cut needed?

- *Access to office:* Is there a clear path to the office doorway and into the office? Is there a ramp? Is the ramp steep, or does it meet the slope requirements? If it includes turns, are the turning platforms at least 60 by 60 inches? Is there a step-up lip into the office, or is the threshold level? Are there any protrusions that could be a hazard to someone who is blind?

- *Controlled access:* If there is controlled access to the property and/or rental office, is the phone or buzzer system low enough to reach from a wheelchair? Could a vision- or hearing-impaired person use it?

- *Elevators:* If there is an elevator to the office, is it usable by the blind? By someone in a wheelchair?

- *Office entry door:* Is the office entry door wide enough for a wheelchair, and does it have a levered door handle instead of a round knob? Is it hard to open? Is the handle no higher than 48 inches? Is there less than 5 lbs. of pressure needed to open the entry door? Does an automatic door remain open long enough for a wheelchair to pass through?

- *Office restroom:* If there is a bathroom available to applicants in the office, is it accessible and usable by someone in a wheelchair? Is there an accessibility sign? With the required Braille symbols? Is the lavatory usable by someone in a wheelchair? Is the faucet levered? Are the hot water pipes under the sink wrapped with insulation material?

This should give you an idea of some of the things to look for when making sure your rental office and other public areas are accessible. If you need guidance, we can direct you to ADA consultants who can assess your needs and make recommendations. Federal ADA information is readily available on the internet at the Department of Justice website: www.usdoj.gov. If your property was built prior to 1990, the important thing is to have an accessibility plan that you are actively implementing. Because the access provisions are complicated, we don't recommend that you try to determine your compliance requirements yourself. This is because inexperience can lead to spending money on changes that don't satisfy the technical requirements for your particular property or may solve a problem but create another problem. For example, someone inexperienced may realize that they need to install a ramp but will have it built with an improper slope, incorrect handrails, or may install the correct ramp but create a problem with the "landing" at the bottom of the ramp. Again, this is where a certified access specialist would be very helpful to you.

Since the federal ADA has already been in effect for over twenty years, you probably won't get a warning from the federal government; in fact, there is no requirement to do so. Consequently, if you receive a complaint, it's critical to contact us immediately because

1. You may have some opportunities to limit damages that a plaintiff can claim; and

2. In cases where you have a certified access specialist report, you can implement a process that can limit exposure, litigation costs and attorney's fees—depending on the facts.

California law: A brief warning that the California Building Code, found in Title 24, also requires accessibility features that, in some instances, don't always conform to the federal ADA requirements. Note that when the California Building Code or the ADA conflict in terms of technical requirements, you are required to select and implement the standard which best promotes disabled access. This makes it all the more important that the property be inspected by a CASp who is knowledgeable about the ADA and California requirements.

Previous law allowed attorneys to make monetary demands along with the initial contact alleging a violation of construction-related accessibility claims under the California ADA or California Building Standards Code. However, the law now prohibits monetary claims in such initial demands. It requires the attorney to include his/her state bar number on the demand letter and to file copies of the initial contact with the CA Commission on Disability Access (CCDA) and the State Bar. Further, the owner of the property is entitled to be provided, in "plain" language, the basis for the accessibility claims.

This law makes "drive-by" lawsuits harder to pursue under the California ADA or California Building Standards Code (although they are still allowed under the federal ADA). Instead, a person with a disability must have actually visited the business and been prevented from accessing the site because of the alleged violations. There is also language that is designed to curb what is known as "stacking" of multiple claims, which occurs when a person with a disability visits the same site on multiple occasions for the sole purpose of increasing their "per occurrence" statutory damages.

Service animals under the ADA's 2010 Amendments: If a person with a guide miniature horse comes into your rental office, don't ask him or her to leave the horse outside. These animals are now acceptable as "service" animals in businesses to which the public is invited. *Note that they have already been accepted in private rental property as disability accommodations for several years under fair housing law.* ◆

Advertising

Businesses advertise to sell their products or services. YOU advertise to market your properties and attract residents. However, there can be a fair housing issue if the advertisement demonstrates a preference or limitation on the type of resident you seek to attract. For example, *before* the California Supreme Court's decision in 1982 concluded that denying housing to families with children was discriminatory, rental advertisements in California could legally show a preference for adults by saying "adults only" or "no pets or children." *After* the court's ruling, these ads became illegal. It was followed by the Federal Fair Housing Amendments Act of 1988, which added familial status to the federal protected classes, making all such ads illegal in all states.

How can you make sure you are advertising as safely as possible from a fair housing perspective? In general, there are four key guidelines:

1) Avoid using any words or phrases that directly or indirectly refer to a protected class or that might indicate to someone that he or she might not be welcome based on membership in a protected class.

2) Focus your advertising on the features, amenities and benefits of your property.

3) Avoid references to the people living in your property or the type of people you would like to have living there. Take a close look at any photos you might be using in your promotional materials. Do they show a potential preference for a certain race, age, nationality, or other protected class? Show that ALL applicants are welcome at your property and that qualified applicants will be approved.

4) Market affirmatively. You are expected to reach out to those who wouldn't ordinarily know about the opportunities at your property.

Use of human models
Brochures and advertisements
After the Federal Fair Housing Act was passed in 1968, it was no longer legal to state in an ad, "white only" or "colored only." Those who wanted to get around the new law then tried to achieve the same goal by using *pictures* instead of words. Display ads in newspapers and promotional materials would show white models almost exclusively. The few persons of color pictured in the ads were shown in subservient positions, such as maids or waiters.

In 1972, HUD adopted a regulation to prevent this activity, later strengthened in 1980. It declared whenever human models are used, they must be representative of the larger geographic community, and shown in an equal social setting. Therefore, if you decide to use human models, make sure there is diversity and equality in your ad campaign.

Use of resident photos
If you post photographs of your residents enjoying community events (such as pool or holiday parties) on bulletin boards, on your property's website or social networking websites[1] or in promotional binders that may be seen by applicants, make sure the residents depicted are diverse. These photos are also considered to be advertising for your property. When applicants do not see anyone in your photos similar to themselves, they are less likely to apply to live at your property.

Display ads
Display (picture) ads for property for rent or for sale in rental magazines, newspapers, rental publications or internet advertising (including your company's and/or specific property's website) should also show representative diversity when using human models or clip-art, as mentioned above. To avoid any potential problems, many companies have decided to simply use pictures of the property rather than human models. It is also recommended that you include the fair housing logo in your display ads.

Use of words
Advertising in general
Make sure your wording in all of your promotional materials is non-discriminatory. Don't mention a protected class or describe the people who live there (such as "professionals" or "active") or describe the people who you want to live there. Instead, focus on the property's benefits and features. Make it clear to the reader that anyone who is interested is welcome to apply.

Classified ads
While fewer print ads for rentals are being placed in print publications these days, if you do use them as a marketing tool, use caution. Since they don't include pictures, your primary concern is with the advertising copy.

---

1. Be sure you get the written permission of the residents before posting their pictures on the internet.

As you compose your ad, ask:

- Does it mention a protected class? *(bad)*
- Does it mention people in any way? *(bad)*
- Does it focus on the property itself? *(good)*
- Does it imply that someone may not be welcome without actually saying it? *(bad)*
- Does it mention any nearby religious buildings? *(bad)*
- Does it make clear that anyone is welcome to apply at your property? *(good)*

Internet advertising

All the same rules and precautions apply to advertisements placed on the internet, whether they are on your company's or property's website, a social media website or another site belonging to a third party.

Enforcing agencies and fair housing organizations continue to crack down on the use of discriminatory ads in the electronic media, which is very easily monitored.

Recent lawsuits against websites that list ads placed by owners and managers indicate that it is very difficult to hold the website owner liable, based on the Communications Decency Act, for discriminatory ads that are placed by property owners or managers. However, the person or company that places that advertisement can be held liable and there have been numerous, costly lawsuits against them in recent years.

Website ADA Accessibility for Persons with Disabilities

The DOJ has been considering new rules for website accessibility for businesses since 2010. However, deadlines continue to be pushed back.

The rule being discussed is located at:
https://www.reginfo.gov/public/do/eAgendaViewRule?publd=201710&RIN=1190-AA61

Ultimately, the DOJ seeks to establish new rules called the WCAG or Web Content Accessibility Guidelines. "The WCAG 2.0 contains 12 guidelines addressing Web accessibility. Each guideline contains testable criteria for objectively determining if Web content satisfies the guideline. In order for a Web page to conform to the WCAG 2.0, the Web page must satisfy the criteria for all 12 guidelines under one of three conformance levels: A, AA, or AAA."

We would recommend that management companies with their own websites ensure they are as accessible as possible, with or without specific government intervention. You can find out more about the potential web accessibility guidelines at: www.w3c.org/WAI/Resources. A customizable quick reference to the current Web Content Accessibility Guidelines 2.0 requirements and techniques that may apply to your website is available at http://www.w3.org/WAI/WCAG20/quickref/.

Marketing in telephone calls and office interviews
Remember, there is no difference between what you say orally to an applicant and what you print in an advertisement. Both activities fall under fair housing rules. Carefully consider the words you use. For example, since you can't advertise for quiet adults, you can't *tell* a caller that you prefer to rent to quiet adults. Nor should you ask an applicant at any time, including on the phone, if he or she has children, is married, has a job, has a disability, is a U.S. citizen or any other questions regarding a state or federal protected class.

Things you can and can't say
The following suggestions provide some specific guidance about what is appropriate to say and what isn't, both orally and in a written advertisement. *(Refer also to the section on "Answers to Common Questions" and "Words and Phrases" in the Appendix.)*

Take a moment to consider how your words, both written and oral, may be received. Maybe YOU think your words sound just fine to you, but remember that many persons from protected classes have experienced years of discrimination, not only in housing but in many other areas of their lives. It isn't what you *intend* to say that counts; it is what is *understood* by the applicant. Something that seems insignificant to you can be taken very differently by someone else. For example, in a true life situation, a woman of color applying for an apartment was asked by a manager, "Oh, I love your dress! How can you afford it?"

In other prime examples, promoting your property as a "private community" or "exclusive community" can cause persons from many protected classes to feel they are not welcome. This is because, historically, certain neighborhoods throughout the country have used these phrases as code words to exclude Jews, Blacks, the Irish, Catholics, "Okies" and others. However, saying that an entrance or patio is "private" is perfectly acceptable.

Used in this latter context, it describes the property—it doesn't imply there is a limitation on the type of residents.

Use of words that describe a property
Some owners and managers have the misconception that they can't say in an advertisement that an apartment has a "great view" for fear of discriminating against vision-impaired persons, or that "walk-in closet" might discriminate against persons who are not ambulatory. However, in 1995, HUD issued a memo which clarified that the use of most common descriptive real estate phrases is acceptable. According to that HUD Memo:

"Section 4. Handicap. Real estate advertisements should not contain explicit exclusions, limitations, or other indications of discrimination based on handicap (i.e., no wheelchairs). Advertisements containing descriptions of properties (great view, fourth-floor walk-up, walk-in closets), services or facilities (jogging trails), or neighborhoods (walk to bus-stop) do not violate the Act. Advertisements describing the conduct required of residents ("non-smoking," "no drugs") do not violate the Act. Advertisements containing descriptions of accessibility features are lawful (wheelchair ramp)."

Marketing affirmatively
Affirmatively marketing your property means housing providers should be sure they are not limiting the marketing of their properties in an attempt to attract only "certain" types of residents. Properties with advertising budgets should be reaching out to people who wouldn't otherwise know about the opportunities available.

Generally, the main focal point would be media with broad distribution, such as newspapers and rental publications that reach a wide spectrum of potential applicants. Newspapers are no longer the preferred method of advertising vacancies, having been supplanted by internet advertising. Adding a specialized advertising medium to the general ones already used can be acceptable. For example, your overall campaign might also include ads in non-English language media. However, it would not be acceptable to advertise *only* in a Spanish-language newspaper or *only* on the bulletin board at the local Catholic church, for example, because such limited advertising would attract only Spanish-speaking or Catholic applicants, which could then result in a segregated property—a violation of fair housing law.

Note that any property receiving federal funding (including HOME and other federal loan programs) must comply with Limited English Proficiency (LEP) rules. More information is available on the HUD website at: www.hud.gov.

Use of symbolism in the rental office

The dictionary describes symbolism as "the practice of giving special meaning to objects, things, relationships or events." Therefore, if applicants come to your rental office and see certain items prominently displayed, it may suggest to them that you have a preference or limitation toward certain applicants.

Religious pictures or statues, rainbow flags or white supremacy symbols are just a few examples of items that can have a strong impact on applicants. This can also apply to political symbols or comments if they make your political point of view obvious, particularly considering the current state of politics. Such symbols should be kept out of the applicants' (and residents') sight – and out of your discussions with them. *This also applies to rental office areas located within the manager's apartment.*

Risk of lawsuit

Online rental advertising covers the entire country, making it easy for fair housing groups to monitor "for rent" ads. Most print ads in newspapers are also viewable in their online versions. This means anyone with a computer and internet service has the ability to search for discriminatory ads.

If a complaint is filed against you, the investigating agency or attorney can review your advertising materials to determine if there is a pattern of discrimination. For example, if a complaint is filed based on familial status and all your advertising materials are clearly designed to attract adults, the ads can help to substantiate the complaint.

In a "refusal to rent" case, it is common practice for investigating agencies to review all the advertising for that particular property during the time of the alleged discrimination. And if the advertising shows that there is also a preference or limitation for other protected classes, the complaint or lawsuit can expand to include them as well! For example, in one case, while conducting the investigation of a complaint based on race, the investigator discovered that the advertising was designed to attract adults. They also found there were restrictive rules against children, and as a result, familial status discrimination was added to the complaint.

There are other words or phrases that can be problematic. For example, whenever the word "quiet" is used in an ad, it is usually a subtle indication that families with children are discouraged from applying...and they are therefore less likely to apply.

Another subtle preference can come up if you point out that the apartment community is in a highly-rated school district, if that district is, for instance, known to be a largely white district. Non-whites may view the comment as a way of indicating a preference based on race. ◆

Answers to Commonly-Asked Discriminatory Questions

It can sometimes be challenging to avoid saying something that might be considered discriminatory to an applicant or resident. It's harder still to make sure you don't give a discriminatory answer to an applicant when the applicant asks you a discriminatory question. Usually, the question isn't intended to be a problem—people are interested in knowing as much as they can about the place they may soon call home.

"Do you take children?"
Some callers or visitors may ask this question because they don't want to live where there are a lot of children. But more commonly, people ask this question because they still encounter managers and owners who don't want children living on their properties.

"Adult" housing has been against the law in California since 1982! (Note that *bona fide* senior housing *is* allowed.) If your property is not a senior community, simply say, "People of all ages are welcome here." If you have specific amenities that are attractive to children, this is a good time to add, "In fact, we have a wonderful playground here and a great wading pool."

"Are there many children living here?"
Parents often want to know this. They want their kids to have friends to play with, but you still can't answer their question because you would be providing information about the protected class called familial status. Simply say, "We are an equal opportunity housing provider, and people of all ages are welcome here." If they push further, point out that fair housing law doesn't permit you to keep track of such information or to discuss it.

If they can't understand why you can't tell them about other children, replace the word "children" with a different protected class. For example, would you respond to "Do you have many Hispanics /Muslims/homosexuals/Blacks living here?" Familial status is treated the same in the eyes of the law as any other protected class.

"What kinds of people live here?"
Similar to the previous question, this is usually a curiosity issue. However, some people who ask this don't want to live in a "mixed" community and may be trying to filter out such properties. Again, simply repeat, "We are an equal opportunity housing provider, and everyone who meets our qualifications is welcome to live here." If the applicant pushes, remind him that fair housing law doesn't permit you to keep track of, or to discuss, that type of information.

"Could you show me an apartment that IS next to another family with kids/other Hispanics/other adults/etc.?" *Or conversely . . .*

"Could you show me an apartment that IS NOT next to a family with kids/Asians/gays/etc.?"
First, to do what the applicant has asked is "steering" and is discriminatory. Second, remind people that you don't keep track of such information, and besides, whoever lives there today may move tomorrow. It may be acceptable to disclose that a neighbor is a smoker (or a non-smoker) as an accommodation for an applicant who requests to see an apartment that is not next to smokers because of a disability such as asthma or emphysema (with the understanding that the situation could change at any time).

"Is the property in a safe/high crime/drug/gang area?"
While not a fair housing question *per se*, the answer you give could create a problem. First, if you tell an applicant that you have a safe property and then something happens to him or her, you might be sued for "guaranteeing" that it was safe to live there. Second, if you make a negative comment, the applicant may think you are using this question as an opportunity to discourage them from living on your property...perhaps for a discriminatory reason.

Direct the applicants to the local police department as a resource for crime statistics of a particular area. Additionally, there are multiple internet sites that can provide the applicant with neighborhood crime statistics and related information. *(Note: Recent on-site criminal activity may need to be disclosed to applicants to protect against liability for negligence. Your supervisor will advise you if this becomes necessary. Also, California law requires disclosure of a death having occurred in the proposed housing unit within the last 3 years, so such a disclosure in compliance with the law should not be deemed to be discouraging.)*

"Are the schools around here any good?" Direct the applicant to the school district for information about local schools. Answering this question might be viewed as a means of influencing or discouraging families with children by stating your personal opinion.

One final point
When applicants ask you these types of questions, don't encourage them to "come back" or "drive by later and look for yourself." The reason for this is that the applicant has asked you a discriminatory question and you have just given them a positive response to help them find out what you are not allowed to tell them. ◆

Applications

Rental applications are the backbone of the rental business. Before tenancy, applications are used to gather useful information about prospective residents. The application not only provides data needed for your screening process, but that information is often relied upon when situations arise during the tenancy, such as in the case of an emergency. After tenancy, an application can provide helpful information should you ever need to collect a resident debt.

Properly used, the rental application will be a valuable tool in the successful operation of your property. Improperly used, you may rent to unqualified and irresponsible applicants and/or you could find yourself in fair housing trouble.

Use a legal, updated application
Use an application from a reliable source (such as your local apartment association), or use one that has been reviewed by an attorney who is familiar with state and federal fair housing and landlord-tenant law. Beware of "off the shelf" forms from stationery stores because they tend to be generic to the whole country and often do not conform to California law (even if they claim to conform). We recommend having your application reviewed regularly by a knowledgeable fair housing attorney to keep current with changing laws and interpretations of the laws.

Don't request discriminatory information
Make sure the application doesn't request information that could be discriminatory.

- Don't ask about the applicant's nationality, sex or marital status. Don't mention the word "spouse" or try to get around it by asking about the "relationship" between applicants. Don't use applications that include sections for "Head of Household" and "Spouse" on the same form unless you participate in a subsidized program that requires such information.

- Don't use the word "children" anywhere on the application.

- Don't ask for information that could be considered intrusive and unnecessary, such as the person's social media information. At this point in the process, ask only what you need to know in order to screen applicants and verify that they are who they say they are.

- Don't require a driver's license because not everyone drives, such as some persons with disabilities.

- Don't ask any questions about the applicant's citizenship or immigration status (California law) unless such information is required pursuant to a government subsidy program.

- Don't require the person to provide a U.S. or state-issued ID since this could exclude people from foreign countries. Persons who want to visit the U.S. for limited periods of time may be required to obtain Tourist Visas, but there is no law requiring a person to obtain a U.S. or state-issued ID. Any government-issued photo ID will suffice.

Note that in January 2015, the California DMV began issuing driver's licenses to undocumented persons. California law states it is unlawful to discriminate against a person because he/she holds this type of a license.

To obtain this type of license, the person must provide at least one, and in many cases, two types of foreign government-issued ID and proof that they live in California (such as a utility bill in their name). The DMV has indicated that, if a Mexican citizen presents a Mexican Consular ID card, the DMV will not require a second form of ID because it considers Mexican Consular Cards to be reliable forms of ID, easily verified through the government's E-verify system. This is significant because, in the past, some landlords have been reluctant to accept Mexican Consular cards as valid forms of ID because they felt the cards were unreliable.

- Don't automatically reject an applicant who doesn't have a social security number. There is no law that requires a person from another country to obtain a social security number to live in the U.S. unless they become employed here. If your screening company says they can't run a credit report without the number, find one who can—based on name, date of birth and address. This assures that you are treating each applicant equally.

The Process

Get one application from each adult

Every person 18 years of age and over should complete an application (and pay an application fee). An exception to this rule could be a proposed adult dependent incapable of contracting (for example, a person who is mentally incapacitated).

Emancipated minors should also complete an application (and pay the application fee). Under California law, a minor may be considered emancipated (and therefore has the same legal rights and obligations as an adult) in one of three ways:

    1) by order of the court,

    2) by having a valid marriage now or in the past or

    3) by being an active-duty member of the military.

Be sure to get a copy of the appropriate paperwork showing the applicant is legally emancipated (i.e. a court order, marriage certificate or proof of active-duty military service).

Applications should be fully completed

Make sure each application is completely filled out—no blank spaces. Instruct applicants to fill in spaces with N/A if a question does not apply to them. Look it over to make sure all information is legible. If you can't read something, ask the applicant to clarify what it says. Compare the information on the application with the applicant's government-issued photo ID. If there are differences, note them and ask about the discrepancies.

Offer applications to all prospective residents

Be sure you offer applications to all prospective residents who come to the property. If you offer them only to those applicants you prefer to have as residents or simply offer them only when you remember to do so, you may be accused of discriminating.

Avoid "pre-qualifying" some of the applicants before you have screened their applications, otherwise you are not offering the same treatment to all prospects. If you have given the applicants a copy of your rental criteria and they wish to apply, they should be allowed to do so.

No codes or symbols

Don't make any marks that could be mistaken for discriminatory coding on the applications. A case in point: several years ago, a management company had employees put a "happy face" on all the applications of minority applicants because they didn't want to rent to them. The company paid well over $1M in penalties as a result. And don't draw little pictures of the applicants on the application (or guest card) to help you remember what they looked like! It could be construed as discriminatory intent.

First come, first qualified, first served is the best policy

There are a number of reasons why the policy of "first come, first qualified, first served" is the safest policy when taking applications.

There are only four things that an applicant must prove in order to file a *prima facie* complaint based on refusal to rent:

    1) that the person was from a protected class,

    2) that the person was qualified,

    3) that the person was denied and

    4) that there was an available unit

It is up to management to prove that there was no discrimination in the selection process. Implementing a "first come, first qualified, first served" policy makes it easier to defend a discrimination claim based on refusal to rent.

Note the date and time on the application when it is submitted to you so that you will know the order in which to process the applications and just in case you need to prove the timing later on. For example, if a qualified applicant from a protected class (for example an applicant with a visible disability) claims you selected someone else's application *after* he turned in his application, you will have to defend that your decision in a fair housing investigation.

Avoid the practice of "batching" applications and then selecting the "best" application from the applicants. You may have to prove that your final selection wasn't based on a protected class or that the other applicants who were qualified weren't selected because of their protected class.

Write the date and time of the decision on the application, once it has been approved or denied, This may be important if you need to prove exactly *when* an available dwelling became unavailable, for example, when an apartment was rented in the morning and a later applicant comes by to apply for it. Also do this for applications from applicants who have indicated they are no longer interested in renting from you. That way you can prove that you did not deny the applicant – they indicated they were no longer interested—it was their choice. ◆

Assistance Animals

Many persons with disabilities require the assistance of an animal in order to function daily or to live their lives as fully as possible. Some animals may be formally trained; others may not be. There is no certification requirement[2]. Fair housing laws state that management must provide reasonable accommodations for persons with disabilities. Allowing an assistance animal is a common accommodation. If the disability and need for the animal are not obvious, you may request written verification regarding the need for such an animal from the person's health care provider or other qualified verifier.

Reminder: the HUD/DOJ Guidelines state an acceptable request for an accommodation may be either in writing or oral. Nor does the person with the disability have to be the person making the request. It could be a household or family member or friend, for example.

Types of Animals

There are several basic types of assistive or service animals: guide dogs for the visually impaired; mobility dogs who pull wheelchairs or help with balance and coordination issues and assist in other services; signal dogs for the deaf or hearing impaired; medical alert dogs for persons who have seizures or medical emergencies, and companion animals (also called psychiatric service, support animals or therapy animals) for persons with mental or psychological disabilities. Studies have shown that persons with mental or psychological disabilities greatly benefit by the presence of animals.

---

2. Note that a certificate from a local animal control department or other agency registering an animal as assistive normally does not require any verification that the owner is actually a person with a disability. The department or agency simply takes the applicant's word for it (under penalty of perjury).

To reduce risk of violation, remember these rules:

Rule No 1: Assistive animals are NOT PETS!
They are the "eyes, ears, legs or emotional support" of the person with a disability. Even if your property doesn't allow animals, an assistive animal must be allowed if a person with a disability requires one for disability-related reasons.

Rule No. 2: No pet deposits or increased security deposits.
You may not require a pet deposit (it is not a pet) or increase the security deposit of persons with disabilities because they have an assistive animal. Any damages caused by the animal may be deducted from the normal security deposit at the termination of the tenancy. If damages exceed the deposit amount, you may sue in Small Claims Court for any additional amounts if necessary.

Rule No. 3: Establish reasonable rules of conduct.
The issue of assistive animals is often very emotional and residents commonly hire their own attorneys or promptly file fair housing complaints when problems arise. If you are faced with a problem assistive animal, call a fair housing attorney to discuss your specific situation before taking action. Good rules of conduct (not pet rules) can be invaluable.

If you allow pets and have pet rules, don't cross out the words "Pet Rules" and then call them Assistive Animal Rules. Not only are the rules different, it indicates that you still may consider these animals pets.

- Rules should allow assistive animals to accompany the person with a disability anywhere on the property such as the community room or pool area (although not IN the pool or spa).

- If the resident doesn't clean up after the animal, or fails to care for the animal properly, he or she must be allowed to correct the situation within a reasonable time.

  - If the resident claims droppings don't belong to his or her animal, some management companies are using a DNA testing program that can identify the culprits. Participation in the program would need to be voluntary for residents with disabilities, but can be mandatory for residents with pets. Persons with disabilities should not be charged any fee for participation in the DNA testing program.

- Trained assistance animals are likely to be better behaved than many of your residents. However, most companion animals are untrained. If an animal is creating problems, such as barking incessantly or lunging at other residents, you must address the problem. Give the resident a reasonable amount of time to resolve the situation and come into compliance with the lease (not a three-day notice).

If the animal bites someone or a problem remains unresolved, you may need to ask the resident to replace the animal with a different one. If that fails, you may find it necessary to ask the resident to vacate the premises, but do not do so without legal counsel.

Rule No. 4: You may not restrict the assistive animal to certain types, certain breeds or impose unreasonable size restrictions.
For example, the assistive animal could be a miniature horse, which is becoming more commonly used as guides for the blind. In fact, in 2010, the revised ADA regulations include them as acceptable service animals in public places. We would suggest you not deny a guide miniature horse in a rental without legal consultation. (These animals are the size of a large dog, can be housebroken like a dog, are smart, sturdy and easily trained to assist a blind person, are hypoallergenic and have much longer life spans than the average guide dog.)

There should be no strict prohibitions against types of animals that can be used for assistance such as "exotic" animals. For example, monkeys are exotic animals but are commonly used by persons with debilitating paralysis to perform household services and personal services, such as heating food and feeding the person.

However, a poisonous, illegal or dangerous animal such as a rattlesnake or tiger would not be reasonable. In California, ferrets are illegal to own.

Rule No. 5: More than one assistive animal may be needed
There may be times when more than one animal may be needed. For example, several members of the family may have different disabilities, each one needing different types of assistive animals. One individual could also need two types of animals, such as a therapy animal for depression and a hearing alert animal for deafness.

If you allow pets on the property, it's important to remember that assistive animals are not pets. Even though a resident has two pet cats (which, let's say, is your pet limit), the resident may also need an assistive dog or other animal as an accommodation. If you encounter a situation where a resident is asking to have multiple animals based on disability, you should obtain legal counsel before taking any action to approve or deny the request.

Rule No. 6: Trainers of animals for persons with disabilities are allowed the same accommodation rights in California as persons with a disability.
This means you may not charge pet rent, a pet deposit or increased security deposit if a resident verifies that he or she is currently training the animal in question as part of an official program. It also means the animal-in-training must be allowed to accompany the trainer in all settings as you would a resident with a disability. In some cases, the animal will not belong to the trainer but to the program. A well-known program is Canine Companions for Independence, which has an excellent website that will give you more insight about the entire program at www.cci.org.

What about persons who are training their pets as therapy animals for hospitals and nursing home visits? This practice is becoming more and more common. Hospitals rarely allow an animal to visit patients unless the animals are trained and approved. They must be able to remain calm under all circumstances, not jump up on patients, have impeccable behaviors and meet other requirements. Although this type of animal is not specifically mentioned in the law, if a resident has written documentation that the dog is being trained or already has been trained and is actively involved in a therapy program, it may be wise to assume it should be treated like an assistive animal serving one of your residents with a disability. It may be reasonable to request updated documentation during the tenancy since the owner may cease participation in such a program. Since the verdict is still out on these situations (meaning we are not aware of any court or administrative agency cases involving this type of animal), it ends up being a risk management decision as to whether or not the animals should be treated as assistive animals under fair housing law.

Rule No. 7: Get advice if you aren't sure about how to handle an assistive animal situation.
If you have any question or concern regarding a request to house an assistive animal, get advice BEFORE rejecting an applicant or refusing a request from a resident. If you act first and check later, the damage may be done and you could be guilty of a "failure to accommodate."

Even a delay in making the decision can be considered discrimination, so act quickly. You could also end up approving a request that is unreasonable or not required by law—i.e. allowing a large number of animals to reside in a small apartment or allowing someone with no apparent disability or related need to have an assistance animal, when he or she hasn't provided the proper disability verification.

Who is eligible to have companion animals?

A common concern of owners and managers of rental housing is what to do about a request for a companion animal by a resident who doesn't appear to have a disability. Simply put, if the person's disability and the disability-related need for the animal are **not** readily apparent, you are entitled to written verification of the disability and need for the animal.

Many landlords have noted an increase in the use of online services providing service dog certificates, cards, vests and even verification documentation for persons with emotional support animals. Note that service animal "registry" certificates or ID cards are *not* generally sufficient verification of disability and need. These types of documents can be purchased from various internet websites without the person having to provide verification of disability and disability-related need for the animal.

Additionally, there has been a rise in online services that provide verification of a person's disability or disability-related need. By filling out a form and paying a nominal fee, a medical professional associated with the online company will verify a tenant's disability need for an assistive animal. While some companies conduct a telephonic interview, these verifications are often provided without ever seeing the requestor in person or engaging in any other medical/therapeutic services with the purported patient. The sufficiency of these types of verifications is currently undecided. If you have questions about the validity of any documents provided as verification, get legal counsel.

Breeds/types of assistive animals

Sometimes the proposed assistive animal is a dog from a breed with a reputation for being dangerous and it may not be covered by the property's insurance carriers. Note: if your insurer will not cover certain breeds of animals, even for a person with a disability or a guest with a disability, such as Pit Bulls, Rottweilers or German Shepherds (German Shepherds are still being trained as guide dogs), you may need to remind them that insurance companies also have fair housing liability.

This means that the insurance company must also make exceptions to their normal policies—such as breed restrictions—in order to accommodate the needs of a person with a disability.)

According to the most recent HUD Guidelines on Assistance Animals issued April 25, 2013:

"The request may also be denied if: (1) the specific assistance animal in question poses a direct threat to the health or safety of others that cannot be reduced or eliminated by another reasonable accommodation, or (2) the specific assistance animal in question would cause substantial physical damage to the property of others that cannot be reduced or eliminated by another reasonable accommodation. Breed, size, and height limitations may not be applied to an assistance animal. A determination that an assistance animal poses a direct threat of harm to others or would cause substantial physical damage to the property of others must be based on an individualized assessment that relies on objective evidence about the specific animal's actual conduct -- not on mere speculation or fear about the types of harm or damage an animal may cause and not on evidence about harm or damage that other animals have caused."

Every situation is different. We would normally recommend that you err on the side of caution by accepting the animal with written verification of the disability and the need for it from an appropriate verifying source. If the situation is unusual, it may be better to be safe than sorry. Get competent fair housing legal advice to help you assess the situation and weigh the risks.

Visiting assistive animals

If your community doesn't allow pets, and a resident's guest who has a disability brings his or her assistive animal when visiting, permission should be granted. If the guest appears to be "visiting" all the time and no disability is apparent, it may be appropriate to obtain verification that the animal is required. This helps forestall the girlfriend who doesn't have anyone to care for her dog when she is gone and claims it is her assistive animal. Always obtain legal advice in these situations. ◆

Caregivers

Caregiver, caretaker, live-in aide, or whatever you choose to call the person who lives on the property to provide needed care for a resident with a disability, the presence of this person is considered to be a disability accommodation. This doesn't include caregivers who pro-vide services but do not live on the property. They are considered guests.

Some companies advertise their communities as "independent living" apartments or refuse to rent to persons who cannot live "independently." Many of them have experienced fair housing litigation by doing so because the statement has a discriminatory "effect" on persons with disabilities. It's a denial of housing based on disability. Under fair housing law, any person with a disability who needs assistance can have a live-in aide to help them live "independently."

Here are nine points to consider when a resident requests a caregiver:

1. The caregiver is an occupant, NOT a resident, is not responsible for the rent and should not be added to the lease.

2. The caregiver must follow the same community rules as the resident. If he or she doesn't, the resident is responsible and may have to get a different caregiver if problems persist. If it appears the resident is being intimidated or abused by the caregiver, you may need to involve a family member or contact APS (Adult Protective Services).

3. If the proposed caregiver has minor children, a pet or an assistance animal or wants to move other family members into the unit, it is recommended that you obtain legal advice from a fair housing knowledgeable attorney.

4. The caregiver can be a family member; however, the person must provide actual caregiving services. If they don't provide services, screen the relative as you would any other applicant and add to the lease as a resident if he or she qualifies.

5. In a *bona fide* senior community, a *bona fide* caregiver can be under the age limitations. (Note that under California law, 55+ senior housing has its own complex rules for live-in caregivers. Contact a fair housing attorney with senior housing expertise for advice before adding a caregiver on a 55+ property.)

6. While you cannot choose a caregiver for the resident, it is reasonable to have the caregiver complete a rental application and investigative consumer report authorization. This provides you with basic information about who is living on the property and allows you to check rental history (and, if in subsidized housing, to check criminal and sex offender history).

Some caregivers have created problems such as dealing drugs, having loud parties or moving in multiple family members without permission. If you would not rent to a resident with such a history, you do not have to allow this caregiver to reside on the property. However, you still need to allow a live-in caregiver—just not THIS caregiver. It is not necessary or advisable to run a credit report since credit history is not relevant in this situation.

7. Have a *written "caregiver" agreement* that spells out the obligations of the arrangement between the resident, caregiver and management. Such a form is available by request by contacting our Fair Housing Practice Group at KTSFairHousing@kts-law.com or 800-338-6039 (three versions are available: 1) senior 55+, 2) subsidized and 3) conventional housing, which includes non-subsidized senior 62+ properties).

8. If the resident vacates the premises, the caregiver must also vacate. (If the caregiver fails to vacate, you would still need to use the formal eviction process to remove him/her from the property.)

9. Subsidized and other affordable properties may have additional requirements regarding live-in caregivers. Please contact a fair housing attorney with subsidized/affordable housing expertise before adding a caregiver on a subsidized or other affordable property. ◆

Children's Rules

F amilies with children continue to experience discrimination despite many years of federal and state protections. Familial status complaints make up the third largest category of cases in California after disability and race/color, according to the California Department of Fair Employment and Housing. Some owners and managers still tell prospective applicants that they "don't take children," or "the property isn't really suitable for children," either directly or by conveying the message indirectly.

One of those indirect means is by establishing restrictive children's rules. The law says that all residents should have an equal opportunity to use and enjoy the property. The Code of Federal Regulations, Section 100.50 (2), states that discrimination *"in the terms, conditions or privileges of sale or rental of a dwelling, or in the provision of services or facilities in connection with sales or rentals, because of race, color, religion, sex, handicap, familial status, or national origin"* is prohibited.

Further, the California Government Code also states, in Section 12927 (c) (1), *"Discrimination [. . .] includes provision of inferior terms, conditions, privileges, facilities, or services in connection with those housing accommodations."* Never establish rules that single out children without a review by a fair housing knowledgeable attorney.

Note that this protected class is called "familial status," not "children." When children are given fewer rights, the whole family is affected. When you are establishing new rules or reviewing your existing rules, keep the following guidelines in mind:

- Don't use the word "children" in your rules. Rules should apply to all residents, not just children. *(The only exception is when the rule is solely for the health and safety of the children,* such as the pool rules mentioned below.) Instead of saying, "Children may not play in the flower beds," say, "The flower beds may not be used for recreational purposes."

- Avoid using terms that are obviously directed at children in your rules, such as toys, tricycles, diapers, playing, minors, etc.

- Don't establish a complete prohibition against use of any amenity based on age. For instance, a rule that says children under 5 years of age can't use the pool/spa or children under 18 can't use the fitness center. The only exception is if you have tanning beds as part of your amenities. California law specifically prohibits the use of tanning beds by anyone under the age of 18.

- If you have more than one swimming pool, don't designate one for families with children and one for adults.

- Except on senior properties, don't restrict the hours in which children may use facilities. This rule has been commonly violated in the use of swimming pools and spas. If the pool and/or spa are open from 8 a.m. to 8 p.m., they should be available to all residents during those hours.

- <u>Do</u> post health and safety rules, such as for swimming pools and spas, as required by your state or local ordinances. For example, in California, when there is no lifeguard present for a swimming pool, a warning sign that states *"Children Under the Age of 14 Should Not Use Pool Without an Adult in Attendance"* in at least 4-inch high letters, must be posted. An adult is any person who is 18 years of age or over.

- Don't require the adult to be a parent, guardian or an adult resident. Otherwise, an adult baby-sitter or relative couldn't bring resident children to the pool (or other amenity) while parents or guardians are away. If, for example, the parents work, the children would be excluded from using the pool until after 5:00 p.m. The result would be the same as having restrictive hours of use for children.

- The above requirement also holds true for the use of spas in California unless there is a local ordinance that states otherwise. In addition, a warning sign regarding the risks associated with spa use must be posted. *(See the section on "Common Area Usage" for wording.)*

- Beware of rules that require children to be supervised by an adult at all times (or, for example, when outside their apartments). In *U.S. v. M. Westland (1994),* such a rule was first held to be unjustified and restrictive. Virtually all cases since then have upheld that decision. A children's rule that purports to be based on a health or safety concern must point to **a specific age-related danger** that the rule is designed to protect against. That danger must be provable through statistical evidence. Providing pool supervision protects against the specific risk of drowning. However, requiring general supervision in the common areas does not meet that health and safety criterion.

- Rules that don't allow children to play on the property in common areas have led to many fines and settlements. Enforcing agencies point out that children need to be able to play outside—it's what children do. It may be reasonable to have playground rules to ensure the safety of those using the equipment since playground accidents are a major source of injury for children. Check with the manufacturer to find out what ages their equipment is designed for. Older children can injure smaller children if they play too rough on equipment intended for toddlers.

- Rules that restrict the use of sidewalks or other common areas by children, such as for riding bicycles, tricycles, skateboards or other wheeled toys, can be a problem and should be considered on a case-by-case basis. For example, is the sidewalk wide enough for wheeled toys and pedestrians at the same time, or is it only "one person" wide?

- If you believe the health and safety of the child or others is being compromised, the appropriate action is to contact the police or CPS (child protective services).

- Do not establish a curfew for children under 18. For example, "Children should not be in common areas or on the community grounds before 7:30 a.m. or after 10:00 p.m." Some cities have enacted curfews, but they are for public places, not private property, and the cities have endured litigation and compromise in order to enforce their curfews. If noise is an issue, enforce your quiet hours for all residents, regardless of age.

- Use of fitness equipment and facilities by children continues to be a gray area of the law. Based on recent determinations by DFEH, we suggest that any rule you might have that prohibits or restricts children from using amenities could be considered a violation. Reasonable supervision based on health and safety concerns may be acceptable if the danger can be proved through statistical evidence. Check with the manufacturer of the equipment to see what its safety recommendations are.

  A rule for a fitness center, which is more restrictive than the pool rules, implies that you believe the fitness center is more dangerous than the swimming pool, something that would be difficult to prove. Check with your attorney before attempting to restrict the use any of your amenities based on age.

- Always look at the reasonableness of your rules where children are involved. Not reasonable by *your* standards, but reasonable to a judge and jury—as well as reasonable to an unbiased outsider looking at your rules.

- Management should be prepared to enforce reasonable rules against all violators, including families with children. California landlord-tenant law already holds residents responsible for the actions of all household members and guests. This means, when enforcing a breach of the lease or rental agreement caused by a minor, the adult residents are liable for any resulting damage or injury and may face eviction as a result. ◆

Chilling or Discouraging Applicants

Managers and owners have been known to dissuade applicants from living on their property by making chilling or discouraging comments. Even well-intentioned comments that are true can have that effect. Watch what you say!

Things not to say:

Families with children

- Don't point out every hazard on the property to applicants with children if you don't point them out to all other applicants. It is the parent's or guardian's responsibility to determine if a property is safe for their children. They can see the balconies, the pool or the fact that the community is perched on a canyon's edge.

    o Be aware that, in an effort to be consistent, if you do tell all applicants about all property hazards, they won't know this is your practice. They may think you are doing this to discourage them from renting based on their status as members of a particular protected class and may file a complaint if denied housing.

- "By the way, we don't have a playground and there's really no place for children to play on our property." Don't imply or state that children are not allowed to play anywhere on the property, or warn, "We have a very 'quiet' community," as this comment is often interpreted as "children are not welcome."

- "And by the way, the schools in the area are not very good." Even if they are poor or mediocre, let the parent find this out from the school district.

- "And by the way, we have a lot of trouble with drugs and crime in this neighborhood." Even if this is true, let the parent find out from the police or the internet.

    o If there has been recent criminal activity on your property that would constitute a threat to applicants, for liability reasons, you should consider disclosing that fact to all who apply. Such a directive should come from your supervisor or the owner.

- "And by the way we have very strict rules that we expect the children living here to follow." (The rules should be the same for everyone with the exception of rules based on children's' health and safety only.)

- Don't ask applicants with children to bring in their child's school records as part of your screening process.

- "And by the way, we have mostly adults and older residents living here." Your "warning" will be a clear indication to the family that they won't appreciate children moving in.

Persons with disabilities or elderly persons
- *"Oh my dear...are you able to take care of yourself okay? Can you get up and down the stairs? Do you think it's safe for you to live alone? I can see that you have a serious problem walking? Do you have arthritis?"*

Any protected class
- Don't make any comments that have the effect of discouraging persons from deciding to live in your property. Your job is to sell the *benefits* of living there, not the drawbacks, real or imagined.

   A classic story involves a fair housing case a few years ago in which a manager warned an applicant about a serious roach problem on the property. The applicant elected not to move in based on the disclosure. Later, it was discovered in a fair housing investigation that there was no roach problem. The manager told the story to all minority applicants so they wouldn't want to live there. That is taking "chilling" to new heights!

Review your statements
Pay attention to the standard comments you make when you are with applicants. How do you describe the property? Could anything you say be considered chilling? Do you give the same nondiscriminatory information to all applicants? ◆

Common Area Usage

Common areas are usually defined as those areas of the property that are open to all residents and their guests rather than individual rental units, balconies and private patios. Common areas must be open to all residents, not just able-bodied residents, adult residents, white residents, Presbyterians or any other group.

Rules for the use of common areas are a frequent source of fair housing complaints. When the resident pays the rent, the resident is paying for all members of the household to enjoy the benefits and privileges of living on the property – so you may have to rethink rules about restrictions in the use of common areas.

Pools and spas *(Also see "Children's Rules")*

Get rid of any rules you have that limit children's use of pools and spas, with one exception: Title 22 of the California Administrative Code, Section 65539, requires signage that says *"Children Under the Age of 14 Should Not Use Pool Without an Adult in Attendance"* when there is no lifeguard.

Additionally, Title 24 of the same code, Section 3119B.5, requires a warning sign for the spa that states

"CAUTION

- o *Elderly persons, pregnant women, infants and those with health conditions requiring medical care should consult with a physician before entering a spa.*
- o *Unsupervised use by children under the age of 14 is prohibited.*
- o *Hot-water immersion while under the influence of alcohol, narcotics, drugs or medicines may lead to serious consequences and is not recommended.*
- o *Do not use alone.*
- o *Long exposure may result in nausea, dizziness or fainting."*

There can be a potential health and safety issue for small children because their bodies may not be able to handle the heat of the spa water. If you decide to establish a more restrictive policy than is specified in the warning sign law, be prepared to defend it based on statistical evidence of the specific health and safety risk.

The number of guests: Consider establishing a policy that reasonably limits the number of guests a resident can bring to the pool or spa at one time, rather than their ages. This eliminates a variety of problems that can arise when one resident brings in a large group to use the pool. A reasonable limitation on the number of children who can be supervised by each adult might be upheld as well.

<u>Swim attire:</u> Another problem area is what constitutes appropriate swim attire. You are likely within your rights to prohibit cut-offs, street clothes or thongs from being worn in the pool or spa. There can be a fair housing issue, however, if someone is prevented from wearing a shirt in the pool when she has a medical condition that prevents her from being directly exposed to the sun or holds a religious belief that she should not be uncovered. A garment dedicated to swimming that isn't washed in detergent, is rinsed in clear water and doesn't have buttons or loose threads that could end up in the filter might be a good compromise.

You may want to consider refraining from policies (written or otherwise) that assign specific swim attire to a specific gender (such as a policy requiring males to wear swim "shorts" or "trunks").

Rather than having a policy that prohibits "diapers" from being worn in the pool, thereby restricting use of the amenity by families, it is better to have a policy that states that "incontinent persons may not use the pool unless they wear appropriate waterproof undergarments." Persons of any age can have incontinence problems, so age doesn't have to become an issue.

Parking lots and driveways

While everyone is entitled to use these areas, *how* they are used can be an issue. Parking lots and driveways can be dangerous places and some companies choose to prohibit all recreational activities in such areas. Fair housing enforcing agencies advise us, however, that if there is an area of the parking lot that could be safely used by children and other residents for recreation, they will take that into consideration when evaluating any prohibitory rule. Rules must be fact-specific and based on the layout of each property, and, as always, there are risk management decisions to be made. If you are unsure, obtain guidance from your legal advisor.

Watch your enforcement of rules as well. Several years ago, the management and security guards of one community singled out a group of young black residents who were alleged to be "loitering" in the parking lot and forced them to disband. Meanwhile, they allowed other young, non-black groups to congregate. It cost the defendants over $1.7M to resolve the complaint *(Walker v. Lakewood Condominium Owners Association et al., U.S. District Court, Central District of California, Case No. 93-4531- KMW).*

Laundry facilities

Laundry facilities are meant for resident use only. However, you may encounter a resident with a disability who needs to have a family member or friend help with laundry. You should accommodate the person by allowing the guest to use the laundry facilities on behalf of the resident.

Residents with disabilities should reasonably be able to use amenities such as the laundry facilities. If you have residents using wheelchairs, we recommend that you make sure they can get into the laundry center. If your property predates 1991 and a resident requests a ramp, technically, it is the resident's responsibility to pay for and install the ramp (it will be your responsibility to maintain it). However, it would be a beneficial upgrade / modification to the property if you install the ramp at your expense, even though not required. We would also recommend that you have at least one front-loading washer and dryer with accessible controls. Properties with first occupancy after 3/13/91 require common areas and facilities to be accessible.

Age restrictions for use of the laundry equipment can be challenging as well. Small children have been known to squeeze behind machines and be electrocuted, or even to climb into dryers. On the other hand, many older children are fully capable of doing the laundry for their families. Generally, a key-accessible laundry area may eliminate many of these problems. Get advice from a knowledgeable fair housing attorney before establishing any rules limiting children from being in or using laundry facilities.

Community rooms, courtyards, park or picnic areas

Don't establish use restrictions that could create problems for these areas. For example, if groups larger than 10 people must obtain permission to have a gathering, be sure you do not restrict the usage based on a protected class, for example, allowing residents to use the community room for birthday parties but prohibiting residents from using the community room for a Bible study class or other religious activity.

Sometimes the use of common areas can present new and challenging situations. At one property, a resident came into a manager's office complaining she couldn't use the pool because there was a baptism taking place in the swimming pool and the new parents' entire church had come to participate—just another day in the life of a manager.

General supervision of children in common areas

(This issue is also addressed under "Children's Rules.") Any rules that say, "All children must be supervised by an adult when in the common areas," just won't fly *(U.S. v. M. Westland, 1994)*. If children are making too much noise or damaging the property, address it as a management problem, just as you would do if a group of adults were doing these things. If, however, you feel children are genuinely at risk, call child protective services or the police. Families with children are paying for the full use of the property.

Playgrounds

It may be reasonable to have safe usage rules for playgrounds since a leading cause of injuries to children is playground accidents. Check with the manufacturer to see what ages the equipment is designed for. If you have equipment intended for very small children (i.e., a tot lot), it can create unsafe conditions for small children when older children are playing on the equipment. Therefore, it may be reasonable to exclude older children or children over a certain height. It may also be reasonable to have children under the age of five supervised on the playground to avoid accidents. In all cases, make sure any rule s established for the use of the playground are backed by sound, non-discriminatory health and safety reasons that can be proved through statistical evidence.

Fitness rooms and equipment

(This issue is also discussed under "Children's Rules.") Excluding children under 18 years of age from fitness rooms or requiring that children under a certain age be supervised by an adult in the fitness room may subject you to a fair housing complaint based on familial status. Reasonable supervision based on health and safety concerns may be acceptable if the danger can be proven through statistical evidence.

Additionally, the equipment in a fitness facility can be deemed an attractive nuisance by the courts, not only because children are attracted to the equipment, but because they also may not have an appreciation of its associated dangers.[3]

Before establishing an age-related supervision rule, it may be wise to contact the manufacturer of the equipment. Ask their representative to identify at what age the equipment can be safely used without the supervision of an adult. It is preferable that written material be obtained to support this information. However, if not available, be sure to document the representative's name, the date and time of the discussion and the company's contact information. While this may not provide you with a complete defense to a familial status complaint based on an age-related supervision rule, it would at least show that you tried to take reasonable steps to back up the health and safety issues behind the rule. As for the *presence* of children in the fitness room, it may be difficult to support an age-based prohibition.

---

3. The case of Smith v. AMLI Realty Co. (1993) demonstrates how courts have applied the doctrine of attractive nuisance when it comes to risks posed by fitness equipment.

Avoid establishing rules for use by persons with disabilities, such as requiring a doctor's written permission or requiring that the person be accompanied by an able-bodied person when using the facilities.

Business centers

Some companies want to prohibit children's usage of the business center entirely. Many owners and managers argue that children may use the business center to access pornography on the internet. It is of some assistance to install filters to prevent such access by adults or children. Unfortunately, some users may know how to get around any blocking software that management has installed. For this reason, it may be reasonable to post a disclaimer sign. This sign should inform residents that using the computers to access pornography is not permitted and that anyone found accessing pornographic sites could risk losing their tenancy.

Today, it is common for students of all ages to communicate with their teachers for homework, assignments and other information over the internet almost exclusively. There are going to be times when a home computer isn't working and the computers in your business office may prove to be a life saver.

With the above in mind, residents should be reminded that they are responsible for the use of the computers by all household members and/or guests.

Loitering

A word about having "loitering" rules. They are risky because loitering is likely to mean different things to different people. Dictionaries general define it as:

- To stand idly about; linger without any purpose.

- To violate a law or ordinance that prohibits persons from remaining in a given location without a clear purpose for an extended period of time, especially when behaving in a manner indicating a possible threat to persons or property in the vicinity.

How would you apply a "loitering" policy on your property? If a group of residents (and guests) are creating problems for other residents, such as being excessively noisy or boisterous, then the issue should be the behavior (noise), not the age of the residents.

Behavior that violates the rules should be treated as a management problem. Always make sure you are not being tougher on a group of persons from a particular protected class than you are with other residents. ◆

Community Policies

Community policies or rules are necessary to avoid and control problematic behavior in an apartment community environment or other rental situation. Their purpose is to ensure that all residents can live together in a peaceful, workable manner. Without rules, you would likely have chaos (which you sometimes have anyway when your rules are ineffective or you don't enforce them). For fair housing purposes, there are several points about rules that you should consider.

a. *Business necessity.* There should be a supportable, non-discriminatory business necessity when establishing or modifying each rule.

b. *Non-discriminatory.* Make sure each rule is non-discriminatory. Even a policy that appears neutral may have a "disparate impact" on a protected class, so carefully analyze the effect that applying the policy may have on members of all protected classes.

   - *For example, a neutral-sounding rule that requires minor residents to be accompanied by an adult resident when using the community's amenities. It prevents them from having equal use of the amenities by allowing adult relatives or babysitters to accompany them.*

c. *Disability exceptions.* Remember to make appropriate exceptions for persons with disabilities.

   - For example, it is reasonable to have a rule that forbids pets in the pool area. However, that would impact a person with a disability who needs a support animal in order to use the pool area.

   Be prepared to make an exception to this rule as an accommodation. However, it does not appear to be reasonable to allow the animal in the pool itself for health reasons.

d. *Children.* Don't single out children in your rules except for specific health and safety reasons and only after you have conferred with your attorney.

e. *In writing.* Be sure all rules are in writing. The lack of written rules can result in unequal application and enforcement of policies. Also, you cannot serve residents with notices for breach of covenant for breaking unwritten rules.

f. *Using written rules that are unenforced.* Even if your pool signage, for example, forbids use of the pool by children 5 and under, but you don't enforce the rule—it is still a violation of fair housing law.

g. *Review.* Have your policies reviewed annually by a fair housing-knowledgeable attorney. Things change—both the laws and their inter-pretations. Always have new policies reviewed before applying them.

h. *Document changes.* Document all revised or new rules, noting the date of each change. Never change a rule on one day to suit your purpose and then change it back again the next day.

i. *Communicate to employees.* Communicate the rules—in writing—to all employees to make sure everyone is aware of them and to ensure that everyone is enforcing the same rules.

j. *Communicate to residents.* Communicate the written rules to all residents. A resident can't be expected to follow a rule that he or she doesn't know about. And importantly, make sure you go over the community policies with applicants *before* they sign the lease so there are no surprises.

k. *Enforcement.* Enforce the rules consistently with all residents. Don't be tougher on children or other protected classes.

- *Don't be afraid to enforce a rule just because the rule-breaker is from a protected class.* Always address the violation equally without regard to who the person is.

l. *No favorites.* Don't play favorites. The rule in apartment management is "be friendly but not a friend." As soon as certain residents become your friends, you have a double dilemma. The other residents will believe you are giving preferential treatment to your friends. Also, your friends may expect and request special treatment from you, such as giving them extra time to pay their rent or not having to pay late fees.

m. *Accommodations.* Be prepared to break or bend a policy as an accommodation for a resident with a disability. For example, if all rent is to be paid directly to the rental office, or would normally paid directly on-line, you may allow a resident with a disability to pay by mail or you might go to the resident's apartment to accept the payment depending on the needs caused by the disability.

n. *Document deviations.* Document deviations from your normal enforcement of rules. If a situation beyond your control occurs and you are forced to do something that is not your "norm," write down what you did, when and why you did it and who was involved, in case you need to defend the action. ◆

Complaints, Handling

If you own or manage property, you have to deal with complaints from residents, guests or employees—it goes with the territory. You should have a standard, written procedure in place to process all complaints, whether minor or serious in nature. You want to ensure that everyone feels their concerns are taken seriously and are acted upon in a timely and equitable manner. If you don't take prompt action on complaints, such as sexual harassment or discrimination harassment, you can end up on the wrong end of a lawsuit.

1. Establish a written procedure for handling complaints

- Have a written policy that states you take all complaints seriously, that complaints regarding harassment of any kind will be investigated and that you will do your best to resolve the issue. This includes complaints from chronic complainers and residents with mental disabilities—both of whom can have some complaints that are not based in reality.

- List each of the steps that are to be followed in the procedure. Make sure all employees know and follow the procedure consistently. Supervisors should spot-check to ensure compliance.

- And by the way, let your residents know how best to register a complaint. By email? Through your website? By phone? In a letter?

2. The complaint

- Get the complaint in writing. If this proves impossible, draft a confirming letter that documents the conversation with the complaining party. It should be sent to him or her, outlining the details of your conversation The letter should also state that if the resident's recollection of the conversation is different, he/she should let you know within a reasonable period of time, such as within 10 working days, otherwise, you will assume your letter correctly reflects the details of the complaint.

- Develop and use a complaint form -- either a paper or online form. Get dates, times, details about what occurred, names of witnesses, whatever information will help you to address the issues fully. Include the date the complaint was received.

- If an employee reports that he or she observed harassment of residents or between residents occurring on-site, have the employee document what was observed. Once you become aware of a discriminatory situation, act on it.

- Act promptly. Don't assume a problem will fade away if you procrastinate. Not only can the problem escalate, a delay in taking action can imply that you approve of the behavior or situation or aren't concerned enough to take it seriously. Further, courts have held that if you knew of such a situation but took no action, you have liability.

  o When we say promptly, we mean as soon as you have enough information to move ahead. Don't react without some knowledge of the facts unless it is an emergency situation.

- Let the complaining party know that you have received the complaint and that it is being acted upon promptly. Confirm in writing.

- If there are witnesses to a situation, get their written corroboration.

- Prepare to protect the complaining resident against retaliation if necessary (this could involve assisting the resident in obtaining a restraining order or allowing the person out of his or her lease without penalty).

3. Investigate

- Where reasonable, have employees observe the situation when there are complaints such as excessive noise, smoke, odors or other disruptive behaviors.

- As confidentially as possible, find out if others have had a similar experience or have heard or observed anything related to the complaint. It is wise to hold these conversations in the presence of a second staff member. See if others will put their observations in writing. Document everything.

- If there is no corroborating evidence, continue with your complaint procedure anyway.

- If the police have been called, be sure to get a copy of the police report. (Please note that only the person who called the police can obtain a copy of the report without a subpoena. Ask the person who called the police to obtain a copy of the report and forward it to you for your records.) If you do not receive a copy, one can be subpoenaed during the eviction lawsuit. The police officer involved can also be asked to testify.

- If there appears to be discrimination (or if one of the parties may have a disability) of any sort, this would be a good time to get a fair housing-knowledgeable attorney involved.

- If a mental disability could be involved, a carefully written accommodation letter to the offender from your attorney may be in order. It should be designed to allow the person a reasonable opportunity to come into compliance with the lease, depending on the nature and severity of the problem.

If the complaint involves another resident or employee
- With a witness present if possible, talk to the alleged offender about the complaint. Explain that you have received complaints and point out dates, times, and what allegedly occurred. Protect the confidentiality of the complaining party where appropriate (i.e., health and safety reasons).

- If the alleged offender could be violent, talk to your attorney regarding how to proceed safely.

- Follow up your discussion with the alleged offender with a written memo of the conversation.

4. Take action based on findings

- If you have found evidence that substantiates the complaint, decide what action is appropriate to take. Your response should correspond to the seriousness of the behavior. For example, a noise problem would be handled with less severity than a threat of violence problem. Treat all similar situations the same way to avoid any appearance of discrimination.

- Is a written warning in order? How many warnings do you allow in similar situations? You want to make sure you're not treating some residents more harshly or more leniently than others. If the situation is serious, should the complaining party file a police report? Is an eviction in order?

- All written warnings should be detailed, pointing out the rules that have been broken, the dates, times, how the rules were broken, etc. Make it clear that the tenancy could be terminated if the problem continues.

5. Follow through

- Let the complaining resident know, in writing, the outcome of your investigation. If you are taking action against the offending resident or employee, maintain that person's confidentiality by simply telling the complaining resident that you are taking appropriate action.

- If there appears to be no evidence to substantiate the complaint or if there is nothing that can be done in the situation, let the complaining resident and alleged offender know.

- Serve the proper notices or warning letters if warranted.

- If you need to terminate an employee's job, be sure to discuss the issue with your attorney to avoid an allegation of unlawful termination of employment. ◆

Criminal Background Checks

Criminal background checks involve difficult issues with potential civil rights, privacy and fair housing implications. On April 4, 2016, HUD issued new guidance for all housing providers regarding how the use of criminal background checks could potentially violate fair housing laws. The guidance outlines how using criminal background screening to deny housing can create a disparate impact (discriminatory effect) based on race due to the higher incarceration rates among Hispanics and African Americans relative to their percentage of the total population and when compared against the incarceration rates of non-Hispanic Caucasians.

If Landlords want to use criminal background checks as part of their rental criteria, they have the burden to show: (1) it is necessary to use criminal background checks in order to achieve a non-discriminatory business objective and; (2) there is no less discriminatory alternative. (The "business objective" would presumably be the protection of resident safety and/or property. However, the guidance states that the business objective cannot be prospective in nature. The landlord must prove that the use of the criminal background checks actually accomplishes the business objective.)

The guidance presents multiple factors that should and should not be considered in developing criminal background check policies. For more information, see the article *"Complying with HUD Guidance on Criminal Background Checks"* in the Appendix section of this Encyclopedia.

Based on this guidance from HUD, the only sure way a Landlord can avoid fair housing liability if he/she wants to consider an applicant's criminal history is to limit the policy to exclude only applicants with prior convictions for illegal manufacture or distribution of controlled substances. If a landlord wants to deny an applicant for any other convictions, the landlord must be able to prove that the particular policy is necessary in order to achieve a substantial, legitimate, non-discriminatory interest, and that there is no less discriminatory way to achieve this interest. It is strongly recommended that decisions regarding policies and assessments in this area be made by owners or upper management rather than by on-site employees and that the policies be reviewed by an attorney with expertise in fair housing before implementation.

▶ *We recommend that companies who intend to conduct criminal background checks have their criminal background criteria reviewed in light of the HUD Guidance. Contact the KTS Fair Housing Practice Group at: KTSFairHousing@kts-law.com or (800) 338-6039 for assistance.*

Differential Treatment

The terms "differential treatment" and "disparate treatment" are used to describe actions by housing providers in which they treat persons from a particular protected class differently from others. To avoid this, it is critical to be as consistent as possible in your daily procedures regarding both applicants and in-place residents.

It is wise to review your daily rental practices to see if there are any activities or procedures that could be construed as unequal or "differential" treatment. Also look for procedures that you may be applying inconsistently. These guidelines may be helpful:

During the leasing process

1. Follow a written procedure for each step of the leasing process. What's the first thing you do when an applicant enters the office? How do you greet him or her? Do you stand up or remain sitting down? Or does it depend on who the applicant is? (It shouldn't!)

2. Ask all phone applicants the same non-discriminatory questions.

3. Use the same phone sales techniques and same enthusiastic tone of voice with every caller. Even if you are having a bad day, you still need to follow the normal procedure. Otherwise, the applicant may think you are not interested or may not want him to apply.

4. When you respond to internet inquiries (by email, through your company's or property's website or on social networking sites), make sure you handle each such inquiry/response in a consistent and timely manner. Nothing is easier to test than response times.

5. Provide all applicants with the *same* information about the property and the available units, including rent and security deposit amounts and availability dates.

6. Give all applicants the same quality tour of the property. If the applicant has a disability that prevents this, have an alternate method of demonstrating the property.

7. Offer each applicant the same materials, such as brochures, applications, written eligibility standards and community policies.

8. Offer every applicant the opportunity to be on your waiting list, if you have one, when nothing that meets their needs is currently available.

9. If you place information about your property or photos of your residents on the internet or on social networks, such as Facebook, make sure the information is NOT discriminatory, that the photos show a diversity of residents, and that you have obtained written permission from the pictured residents to place their photos online.

10. Screen each applicant in the same way (using a written checklist to make sure you follow a consistent procedure if you do not use an outside screening service that does the entire process for you). Do not check only on people you think might have problems or only those who look like they might be the best qualified.

11. Notify applicants about their screening results following the same procedure. Applicants who are denied residency (or who only qualify conditionally with a co-signer or additional security deposit) based on information from a credit report must be notified in writing through an adverse action letter including specific requirements when credit scoring systems are used as a basis for denial.

12. Document any deviations from your normal leasing procedures.

During the tenancy

1. Provide the same move-in information to all new residents, the same quality move-in gifts and the same move-in assistance.

2. Handle each resident complaint the same way, using a written procedure.

3. Make requested repairs promptly for every resident, using a written procedure that is consistently followed.

4. Treat every resident's guests in the same friendly and courteous way. This includes children's guests.

5. Have a smile for every resident, not just some. People notice!

6. Enforce your house rules or community policies fairly and consistently for all residents.

When can you provide different treatment?
If screening results show that credit, income or rental history does not allow applicants to be automatically qualified, you don't not have to approve the application.

If some applicants don't fully qualify (such as applicants lacking a credit or rental history), you can require all similarly situated applicants to meet certain conditions in order to be accepted *(conditional acceptance)*, such as requiring them to pay an additional security deposit or obtain a cosigner. As long as these policies are applied equally to all applicants, they should not be considered discriminatory.

If the applicant or resident is a person with a physical or mental disability, you are required by fair housing law to make reasonable accommodations for the person if requested to do so. In most cases, this means adjusting a rule, policy, practice or service in order to allow the person to live on the property successfully. Filling out the rental application for a person who is unable to use his/her hands or allowing support animals when you do not accept pets are simple examples of acceptable differential treatment. (Note that even if you fill out the application, you need the applicant's signature or "mark" to acknowledge they have given you the authorization to screen their application). ◆

Disability: Reasonable Modifications

Until the Federal Fair Housing Amendments Act (FHAA) was passed in 1988, persons with disabilities throughout the United States, particularly those with mobility impairments, were relegated to only a few housing choices. They could compete for the handful of accessible units available, live as shut-ins and rely on others to take care of their needs or live with family members or friends in single-family homes that could be adapted for their needs. Generally, living in multi-family housing was not a realistic option.

Before we delve further into the area of disability, we want to mention that a person should not be defined by his or her disability; consequently, wherever possible it's important to say a "person with a disability" rather than a "disabled person." They are persons first, persons with a disability second. Using appropriate terminology is a good habit to get into when you are discussing disabilities and is greatly appreciated by those who must live with such challenges.

Availability of units to qualified applicants with a disability

Since 1988, ALL units must be made available to persons with disabilities as long as the applicant meets your rental qualifications. In conventional or non-subsidized properties, persons with a disability can select any vacant apartment they like, just like residents without a disability. The unit doesn't have to be on the first floor to be accessible—in fact, be sure you do not encourage someone to rent on the first floor or any other location based on their disability or you could be found guilty of illegal "steering."

Since persons with physical or mental disabilities cannot always perform the same activities in the same way as persons without a disability, they have been given several rights designed to level the playing field. One of those rights is the ability to make reasonable modifications to their dwellings.

Modifying the apartment (For new or existing residents)

Whether a person with a disability is a qualified applicant or a current resident), he or she has the right to make reasonable modifications to the dwelling or common area that would make it accessible so he or she can have full use and enjoyment of the property. The requirements in conventional (non-subsidized) properties include the following:

- The modifications must usually be made at the resident's own expense.

  - An exception would be made in federally-funded housing, subject to Section 504 of the Rehabilitation Act of 1973, where the property pays for the modifications.

  - Another exception would be if your property had first occupancy on or after March 13, 1991, but it wasn't built to comply with the federal Fair Housing Act's construction accessibility requirements. In that case, the owner must pay to bring the property into legal compliance.

  - You may choose to make modifications at your expense when you are not required by law to do so; however, be prepared to do the same for all other residents who need the same modifications.

- The resident must see that the modification is performed in a "workmanlike manner." The law doesn't specify who should do the work. Some changes do not require much skill, such as changing door knobs to levered handles. However, it may be reasonable for a landlord to insist that some work be done by a licensed, bonded contractor, particularly if it requires special skills or a building permit or, in California, if the contractor's fee (including materials and labor) is over $500. The person with a disability must obtain any permits required by law.

- The modifications must be necessary and related to the disability.

- The modifications may not permanently damage the property, such as removing a load-bearing wall.

Management has the right to know what changes are planned and to be assured that the work will be done in an appropriate manner. If management believes the modification is unreasonable (and has supportable reasons), both parties should negotiate and determine whether there is a reasonable alternative that will work for both parties. It is important to document every step of the way.

Establishing the need for a modification (or an accommodation)
It is wise to have a written procedure for handling modification and accommodation requests so you are providing the same opportunities and treatment to all who make requests. However, the HUD/DOJ Accommodation Guidelines (May, 2004) state, *"A provider may not refuse a request, however, because the individual making the request did not follow any formal procedures that the provider has adopted."*

Written or oral requests

When a resident or applicant seeks a modification or accommodation based on a disability, ask him or her to make the request in writing. The courts will uphold an oral request, but a written request is optimal. If an oral request is made and a written request does not appear to be forthcoming, you should put the request in writing and verify with the resident/applicant that your understanding of the request is correct. If possible, ask the person to sign or initial the request.

Sometimes the request may not be made in a direct fashion, but it would be clear to an "average" listener that the person may be indicating that he or she has a disability and needs something. For example, let's imagine that a resident tells you she is having a hard time walking to and from her assigned parking space but she doesn't directly ask you for a different parking space. When this happens, ask if the person needs something, for instance: "Joan, are you asking me for something?"

When verification is necessary

Both the 2004 HUD/DOJ Accommodation Guidelines and the HUD/ DOJ Modification Guidelines (March 2008) state,

"A provider is entitled to obtain information that is necessary to evaluate if a requested reasonable accommodation/modification may be necessary because of a disability. If a person's disability is obvious, or otherwise known to the provider, and if the need for the requested accommodation/modification is also readily apparent or known, then the provider may not request any additional information about the requester's disability or the disability-related need for the accommodation/ modification.

If the requester's disability is known or readily apparent to the provider, but the need for the accommodation/modification is not readily apparent or known, the provider may request only information that is necessary to evaluate the disability-related need for the accommodation/ modification."

For example, if a person uses a wheelchair and wants to widen the kitchen and bathroom doorways in the apartment, no further verification of the disability or need is necessary because both are obvious or apparent.

If that same resident asks if he can install extra electrical lines and a cable line so that he can use computer equipment that helps him communicate with others, the need may not be apparent unless you are aware that he is also hearing impaired. Otherwise, the need for the extra electrical and cable lines is not apparently related to the disability that confines him to a wheelchair. In that case, you may request verification of the disability-related need for the requested modification.

Obtaining verification of the disability

The HUD/DOJ Guidelines include several other sources of potential verifiers, besides health care providers:

"Depending on the individual's circumstances, information verifying that the person meets the Act's definition of disability can usually be provided by the individual himself or herself (e.g., proof that an individual under 65 years of age receives Supplemental Security Income or Social Security Disability Insurance benefits or a credible statement by the individual). A doctor or other medical professional, a peer support group, a non-medical service agency, or a reliable third party who is in a position to know about the individual's disability may also provide verification of a disability."

While most verifications continue to come from doctors and medical professionals, if another type of credible verification is presented, do not automatically deny the request. If it comes from one of the sources listed below, it must be considered. If you are unsure, obtain legal counsel.

- A peer support group could involve veterans with PTSD, persons with mental illnesses, or an alcohol or drug-related self-help group for recovered alcoholics and drug addicts.

- A non-medical service agency could be a local chapter of an MS Society or the Alzheimer's Association that provides programs for persons with those disabilities or an agency that supplies in-home caregivers or other support services.

- A credible third-party could be the person's case worker or even an agency that is providing the person with a service animal.

- A self-statement by the resident, such as receiving income from SSDI or SSI if under 65 years of age, or, if requesting an assigned parking space, a state-issued handicapped license plate or placard.

The three areas to be verified include:

1. In the verifier's opinion, the person meets the California definition of disability; AND

2. The requested modification or accommodation relates to the disability; AND

3. The person requires the requested modification or accommodation in order to have full and equal use and enjoyment of the property.

Do NOT make any inquiry into the nature or severity of the person's disability. Do NOT contact the health care provider to ask questions about, or obtain additional information about, the person's disability. Remember that any information provided should be for the purpose of verification only, must be authorized by the person with a disability and must be kept strictly confidential.

Establishing reasonableness

Your job is to determine if the requested modification or accommodation is reasonable. The modification (or accommodation) may be deemed unreasonable if it imposes **undue** financial or administrative burdens on the landlord or alters the fundamental nature of the business (providing housing). If an applicant or resident makes a request that you feel is unreasonable, you are expected to *open a dialogue and negotiate with the person (participate in the "interactive process")* to try to come to a workable solution. It is not recommended that you deny the request unless you have discussed it with an attorney. Over 20% of all complaints filed in California are based on denial of an accommodation or modification.

When the resident with a disability resident moves out

When the person moves out, he or she can be required to restore the modifications made to the interior of the dwelling to their original condition (except for normal wear and tear) at his or her expense if it is reasonable to do so, to the extent that the modification would negatively affect the next resident, who does not have a disability, and make it difficult to lease. For example, widened doorways would not affect the next resident, but lowered kitchen cabinets would be a problem.

In very limited circumstances, the law allows the owner to require the resident to pay, over a period of time, into an interest-bearing escrow account to ensure adequate funds will be available to make the restoration. The interest earned on the escrow account accrues to the benefit of the resident. According to the HUD/DOJ Guidelines issued in March of 2008, the decision to require an escrow account *"should be based on the following factors: 1) the extent and nature of the proposed modification; 2) the expected duration of the lease; 3) the credit and tenancy history of the individual tenant; and 4) other information that may bear on the risk to the housing provider that the premises will not be restored."* It is recommended that you consult with an attorney before making a decision to require the establishment of an escrow account.

What about ramps?

Generally, the resident is responsible for installing ramps where required to gain wheelchair access to his or her apartment or the common areas in non-federally-funded communities. In new construction with first occupancy on or after March 13, 1991, there are accessibility requirements for common areas, as well as for the dwellings, and a ramp should be unnecessary if the property was built in compliance.

The owner may be wise to offer to voluntarily make the installation in order to control quality, aesthetics and safety of the ramp. For older properties, the owner may find it to be a beneficial upgrade/modification to install all needed common area ramps, such as access to the laundry facilities, swimming pool area and recreation room, as an accommodation.

If the resident has installed ramps anywhere outside his or her unit, he or she is not required to remove them when vacating.

In government-assisted properties that are subject to Section 504, the property is normally responsible for installing a needed ramp.

Modification upgrades

If a modification (for example, a ramp to the fitness facility) would ordinarily cost the resident $1,000, but the landlord wants it upgraded to make it more aesthetically pleasing, the landlord would be required to pay the additional cost of the upgrade.

Maintaining modifications

If a modification is used only by the resident, he or she is responsible for maintaining it, such as a ramp to his or her own unit's front door.

If the modification is also used by other residents, such as a ramp to the laundry room, the property is responsible for its maintenance and the costs associated with the maintenance. ◆

Disability: Reasonable Accommodations

One of the special rights afforded to persons with disabilities is the right of reasonable accommodation. Specifically, CFR §100.204 states: *"(a) It shall be unlawful for any person to refuse to make reasonable accommodations in rules, policies, practices, or services, when such accommodations may be necessary to afford a handicapped person equal opportunity to use and enjoy a dwelling unit, including public and common use areas."* Accommodations tend to vary on a case-by-case basis.

Accommodations involving community policies

The most common accommodation is a change, exception or adjustment of a community policy that would otherwise prevent the person with a disability from full use of the property. For example:

- Permitting the person to have a support or assistive animal (including companion animals) even though you have a "no pet" policy,

- Permitting guests of the resident to use the laundry facilities on his/her behalf even though you have a policy prohibiting guest usage,

- Permitting a guest with a disability to bring an assistance animal to visit a resident even though there are pet restrictions on the property,

- Permitting a support animal to accompany the resident in the pool area or community room even though you do not permit other animals there (but arguably not IN the pool because of health and safety concerns),

- Assigning a parking space close to the person's dwelling or

- Mailing, faxing, emailing or delivering an application to an applicant with a disability who is unable to leave his/her present apartment.

An accommodation *could cost* management some money. (The amount of money considered reasonable for an accommodation tends to depend on the assets of the owner/company.) Examples of such accommodations include

- Installing automatic shut-off faucets for persons who suffer from memory loss and may otherwise leave water running.

- Installing flashing smoke and carbon monoxide detectors for hearing-impaired residents who would not hear a standard alarm.

- Designating a reserved spot with white striping and signage for a mobility-impaired resident. Note that reserving a space for such a resident is a separate issue from the designation of blue-striped handicap spaces for the public under the ADA.

- Adjusting the door to the fitness room to make it easier for a person with a disability to open.

Financial accommodations

Allowing a co-signer/guarantor: In recent years, there has been a growing trend toward requiring that landlords consider "financial accommodations." This trend began with the case of *Giebeler v. M & B Associates, September 15, 2003.* In the Giebeler case, the court found that the landlord acted improperly in denying Mr. Giebeler's request for a reasonable accommodation in the form of allowing him to have a co-signer in lieu of meeting the property's rent-to-income ratio (the property did not allow co-signers). A full explanation of this important Giebeler case is found in the appendix to this Encyclopedia.

Modifying rent due-dates: Since the time of the Giebeler decision, there have been additional cases in which courts and/or enforcing agencies have found that housing providers must consider modifying a financial policy in order to accommodate the needs of a resident with a disability. For instance, allowing a person with a disability whose sole or main source of income is from disability payments to pay his or her rent on a date that coincides with the date the disability checks are received from the government.

Third party checks/payments: Another example would be accepting a social service agency's checks or auto pay as payment for the rent of a resident with a disability. Sometimes agencies that provide services for persons with disabilities will also make financial assistance available. (Note that this is different than accepting monies from a housing authority as part of the Section 8 program and also is different from corporate-style rentals where an agency may lease a unit and then place persons with disabilities in the unit.)

Transferring to another unit: Another example would be allowing a resident with a disability, who lives in an upstairs unit, to transfer to a same-size ground floor unit at the same monthly rental rate the resident was paying for the upstairs unit—even though the downstairs unit may currently rent for more money than the upstairs unit.

Would the above accommodations pose an undue burden on the landlord? One of the tests that will be applied in order to determine the reasonability of these types of request is —does it impose an ***undue*** financial oradministrative burden on the landlord? Using the example directly above, advocates could argue that once the resident vacates the upstairs unit, the landlord could then re-rent that unit at the higher price—thus negating any undue financial burden.

Acceptance of Section 8 Housing Choice Vouchers (HCV): There was a California case in which the resident's attorneys argued that a landlord should have to accept a Section 8 voucher as a reasonable financial accommodation for disability, despite the fact that the landlord does not participate in the Section 8 program. Although the trial and appellate courts in this matter ruled in favor of the landlord, the ruling was very specific to the particular facts of

---

that case. Tenants' rights and other advocacy groups are continuing to argue that acceptance of Section 8 should be a reasonable accommodation when the person can show that, but for the disability, he/she would not have to be on Section 8. It is likely that any future case will revolve around whether participation in the government program would constitute an undue burden.

Recommendation: If you are faced with a situation where a resident is requesting a financial accommodation, it is recommended that you consult an attorney who is well-versed in this cutting-edge area of fair housing law before making any decision to grant or deny the request.

The request and verification
Please refer to "Written and oral request" in the previous section on "Disability: Reasonable Modifications" for the federal HUD/DOJ Guidelines on handling requests and verification.

- Reminder: if the disability is obvious or known (such as financial verification in the file that the person's income is from a disability-related source such as SSI or SSDI), no verification of disability is necessary. If what is being requested obviously relates to the disability, no further verification of need is necessary. If either the disability or need is not obvious, verification may be required.

- If the person is obviously visually impaired and has a guide dog, no further verification is necessary.

- If a person with a handicap license plate requests an assigned parking space, no further verification is necessary.

  If the person or household member who wants an assigned space doesn't appear to have a disability and doesn't have disabled license plates but only has a placard, you should be able to ask for the paperwork regarding the placard to be assured that the placard belongs to that person.

- If a person doesn't appear to have a disability and wants an animal in a pet-free property, you may ask for verification of both the disability and need for the animal.

Reasonableness

As with modifications, management has the right to determine if the request is reasonable. If it 1) imposes an **undue** financial or administrative burden on the landlord, 2) fundamentally alters the nature of the operation or 3) creates health and safety risks that make it unreasonable, you are expected to negotiate with the person to come to a workable resolution. For example, it wouldn't be reasonable to assist the resident with his medications or housekeeping, run errands for him, give him a ride to the doctor's, or feed and walk his assistance animal because you are not operating an assisted-living community. But the resident should be allowed to get a caregiver if that is an alternative that would meet his needs.

The determination of undue financial and administrative burden must be made on a case-by-case basis. Considerations include the cost of the requested accommodation, the provider's financial and personnel resources, the benefits that the accommodation would provide to the person with the disability and if there are alternative accommodations that would effectively meet the person's needs.

A landlord should not take into consideration an expectation that if one accommodation is granted, others might be requested. Each request should be analyzed separately on its own merits.

Again, we would recommend that you not deny a request unless you have discussed it with an attorney. Denial of an accommodation is a leading cause of discrimination complaints.

When other residents ask why . . .

If other residents ask you why a resident with a disability is getting a special parking place or animal or other accommodation, particularly when the disability is not obvious, simply say "We appreciate your concerns, but in this situation, we are following all state and federal laws." Avoid mentioning "fair housing laws" or it will be obvious that the person has a disability which is deemed confidential information.

Another useful response is, "Just as I wouldn't discuss anything about you with our other residents, I cannot discuss anything about another resident with you."

Accommodating persons with a mental disability

When faced with someone with a mental illness, it is a common reaction to want the person off the property so you don't have to deal with anticipated problems. However, an accommodation is almost always in order.

To help you better understand your responsibilities, let's look at three levels of possible behaviors that may cause concern:

Level 1. *Behaviors that are irritating and bothersome, but are harmless.* Generally, landlords have a conversation with the person about the behavior and document it by writing a confirming letter. The person's emergency contact can be called upon for assistance. However, take care to maintain as much confidentiality as possible, or to get the resident's written authorization to communicate with the contact person.

Level 2. *Behaviors that are lease violations.* Level 1 behaviors can rise to the level where action needs to be taken. Don't automatically give the person a notice to move or a 3-day notice to perform covenant or move. You must make a reasonable attempt to accommodate the person's disability. Let the person know, in writing, what the lease violations are and that you will give the person a reasonable time to comply with the lease. Depending on the circumstances, a reasonable time could be several weeks or more. All violations and actions taken should be well-documented. You want to be able to demonstrate that you have made every effort to accommodate the person's behavior.

Level 3. *Behaviors that create a health and safety risk or direct threat to the other residents and property.* If you believe this to be the case, you would be wise to obtain legal advice before taking action. Except in extreme cases, you must make a reasonable attempt to see if there is some accommodation that will eliminate or sufficiently mitigate the direct threat.

A good faith effort may also mean consulting with family members, caseworkers, health professionals, agencies or other resources to find a resolution—*maintaining as much confidentiality of the person's disability as possible.*

If, after making a good faith attempt to reasonably accommodate the person, you find it is not working, or if the person continues to pose a threat to the health and safety of the other residents and/or property, you may need to proceed with an eviction. Do so only after obtaining legal advice.

If the mental disability causes a severe health and safety threat, you and your attorney need to consider the premises or personal liability issues for other residents, as well as fair housing issues. Termination of tenancy should come only if there is no reasonable accommodation that will eliminate or acceptably minimize the threat. ◆

Disparate Impact or Discriminatory Effect

Normally, we think of discrimination as something a person does intentionally. However, you can be sued for discrimination even though you didn't realize you were discriminating and didn't intend to do so. The end result of an unintentional discriminatory act is still discrimination in the eyes of fair housing enforcement agencies and the courts—someone received unequal or unfair treatment because of their status as a member of a protected class.

Although the issue of disparate impact has been used in many discrimination cases over the years and upheld in multiple federal courts, it hadn't been specifically spelled out in federal fair housing law. It has been a part of California's FEHA (*Government Code 12955.8 (b)*) for many years.

In early 2013, HUD established a new Regulation (Subpart G—Discriminatory Effect -- §100.500 Discriminatory effect prohibited) which defined a housing practice with a "discriminatory effect" as one that "actually or predictably:

(1) Results in a disparate impact on a group of persons on the basis of race, color, religion, sex, handicap, familial status, or national origin; or

(2) Has the effect of creating, perpetuating, or increasing segregated housing patterns on the basis of race, color, religion, sex, handicap, familial status, or national origin."

In simple terms, this type of discrimination occurs when a policy or practice that appears neutral has the "effect" of discriminating against a person or persons from a protected class.

In June, 2015, the U.S. Supreme Court, in a 5-4 decision, ruled in support of "disparate impact" in the case of Texas Department of Housing and Community Affairs v. Inclusive Communities Project. The ruling endorses the notion of citing disparate impact in housing cases under the federal Fair Housing Act, meaning that statistics and other evidence can be used to show decisions and practices have discriminatory effects, without proving that they're the result of discriminatory intentions. Since this ruling, disparate impact has received increased national attention, particularly from HUD which, in 2016 has released several pieces of new guidance related to this concept, focusing on issues concerning criminal background checks (*For more information, see the section on criminal background checks*) domestic violence, and limited English proficiency (*For more information, see the section on limited English proficiency*). There is a test used to determine if a policy or practice that has a disparate impact or discriminatory effect may still be reasonable.

California

The California FEHA states, "A business establishment whose action or inaction has an unintended discriminatory effect shall not be considered to have committed an unlawful housing practice in violation of this part if the business establishment can establish that the action or inaction is necessary to the operation of the business and effectively carries out the significant business need it is alleged to serve.

In cases that do not involve a business establishment, the person whose action or inaction has an unintended discriminatory effect shall not be considered to have committed an unlawful housing practice in violation of this part if the person can establish that the action or inaction is necessary to achieve an important purpose sufficiently compelling to override the discriminatory effect and effectively carries out the purpose it is alleged to serve."

HUD

The HUD Regulation states "that a 'legally sufficient justification' exists where the challenged housing practice:

(1) has a necessary and manifest relationship to one or more legitimate, nondiscriminatory interests of the respondent or defendant; and

(2) those interests cannot be served by another practice that has a less discriminatory effect."

When making rental decisions, ask the question "Is there a less discriminatory way to achieve this necessary business goal?" If there *is* a better way to achieve it, there may be a fair housing violation.

Let's look at a simple example that demonstrates this principle. A familial status complaint was filed against a property based on its occupancy standard. The property had all two bedroom units with an occupancy standard of no more than three persons per apartment. The reason for the standard, according to the property management company, was the limited number of parking spaces available.

The occupancy guideline generally used by the California Department of Fair Employment and Housing (DFEH) is a minimum of two persons per bedroom plus one for the unit, allowing up to five persons in a two-bedroom apartment. (A higher occupancy standard can usually be established at the landlord's discretion as long as it does not violate the Uniform Housing Code.

Those laws generally require only that there be a certain number of usable square feet per person and usually allow more occupants than the DFEH guidelines.) Occupancy standards that are less than the state minimum guideline may have a disparate impact or discriminatory effect on families with children as well as ethnic groups that may commonly include extended families. In other words, a lesser standard, although based on numbers, not types of people, has a tendency to keep families out.

When we apply the test to this case—was there a less discriminatory way of resolving the limited parking situation?—the answer is yes, by limiting the number of vehicles that can park on the property. The limited occupancy standard had a disparate impact on families with children and was therefore a violation because *there _was_ a less discriminatory way* of handling the parking problem.

Two other common examples of disparate impact include:

- A policy that requires all residents to make their rent payments on-line or through direct deposit could impact a person with a disability if their disability makes that difficult or impossible. California Law explicitly prohibits landlords from requiring that rental payments be only made via electronic funds transfer (Civil Code 1947.3).

- A policy that doesn't allow applicants to use co-signers or guarantors in order to qualify for an apartment could impact students (age), persons with disabilities, persons from other countries (national origin) or those from other protected classes who may meet all but one of your standards.

As a practical matter

When establishing or reviewing rules or practices, stop and ask if any of them could impact one of the protected classes. Your most vulnerable documents (policies and procedures manual, rental criteria and community rules) should be reviewed for issues that place you at risk for potential violations. ◆

Documentation

We cannot overstate the importance of good documentation when it comes to fair housing. It may be the only thing protecting you from a huge settlement, fine or award in a discrimination case.

Ask anyone who has been through a fair housing investigation. Unlike most legal situations, you are often considered guilty until proven innocent in fair housing cases. Without documentation, the investigator, hearing officer or judge must rely on verbal recollections that may be hazy at best. Courts, in the absence of concrete evidence, tend to go with the underdog because you, as owner or manager, are in the controlling position. Even a small owner/operator is still perceived to be a business person.

What kinds of documentation should you keep? The following list will provide you with an overview of a defensive documentation program that creates an invaluable paper trail should you need one.

If your company has transitioned into being paperless or if most documents are entered or scanned into the computer, you will still need to be able to print out the necessary documents if there is a lawsuit or fair housing complaint. A judge won't be interested in looking at your laptop.

LEASING DOCUMENTS
Keep all documentation for a minimum of three, preferably four, years after the tenancy ends. This includes denied applications.

1. **Advertisements.** Copies or samples of your ads or ad campaigns, including where the ads were placed and when, should be kept. If you offer a rent special, keep copies of the promotion and the dates the specials began and ended.

2. **Applications.** Both accepted and denied applications should be retained. Make sure they do not request any illegal information. Include supporting documentation that explains the reasons for acceptance or denial. We do not recommend you take a copy of a photo ID before approval of an application, in case the application is denied and the applicant claims that the denial was based on the way he or she looked.

3. **Leases, agreements and all addenda.** Keep these documents, signed by the Resident, in your files for four years after the contract ends, for use in a potential breach of contract defense case.

4. **Screening and verification records.** Include who you talked to, what they said and when they said it. A check-off list that shows this information is useful. This includes credit reports, screening company results, employment or other income verification, written rental history references from previous landlords, adverse action letters, etc.

5. **Guest cards.** They may be your only written history of visits by applicants that didn't result in the submission of an application. The best evidence is a guest card completed and signed or initialed by the prospective applicant. Second best are those completed by the leasing agent and initialed or signed by the prospective applicant. Note what he or she was looking for, what units were shown and any objections raised by the applicant. If your guest cards are entered directly into the computer, you still may need to provide a printed copy at a later date.

6. **Traffic logs.** Not everyone who visits completes a guest card. For all other foot traffic, have a system for noting the date, time, gender, number of persons, subject of visit (if known), etc.

7. **Availability logs.** These can be critical if it becomes necessary to prove what units were available on a given date. They usually list what was available when and at what rate, dates and details of any rent specials and special features of the rental unit.

8. **Rental criteria.** Back up your rental standards by documenting your non-discriminatory business reasons for establishing each of them. Be sure the standards have been reviewed by a fair housing attorney because they are a frequent source of fair housing problems!

9. **Phone logs.** Always maintain a log of incoming and outgoing calls with prospective residents, whether it is on paper or on a computer. Never use "post-it" notes as your phone records. Yes, that still happens!

TENANCY DOCUMENTS

1. **Community policies.** Back each policy with written, non-discriminatory reasons for its establishment. Note the date each policy was established or modified and when it went into effect.

2. **Maintenance requests and maintenance records.** Your service requests should ask enough information to do the job right the first time. Document all actions taken for each request.

3. **Incident reports.** What happened, who was involved, date and time, witnesses, conditions (such as "wet because of rain"), actions taken at the time of the incident and any follow-up that was taken

4. **Notices.** Any notices served on residents.

5. **Rent rolls.** Ongoing records of rent payments, late fees, increases, lease start and end dates, etc., for every unit.

6. **Correspondence (internal and external).** Memos to residents, warning letters, lease renewal or nonrenewal letters, letters from attorneys or fair housing agencies, disability requests and verifications, as well as letters received from the resident.
   Also keep letters, emails and memos that the owners or management personnel have written to each other regarding the resident.

7. **Complaints.** Keep notes taken during phone calls from complaining residents. Maintain all written complaints from residents or confirming letters if residents were unwilling to put their complaints in writing. Confirming letters are written by management to the complaining resident, describing the situation as understood by the manager. It requests that, if the manager's understanding is not correct, the resident should make any corrections within a reasonable time (i.e., 10 working days).

8. **Conversation logs.** Keep a written on-going log, either on paper or in a computer file that provides a chronological record of all contacts by all members of the management team with the resident in each resident's file. This can provide vital evidence in a fair housing case or an eviction.

9. **Registers or journals.** Keep track of any notable activities occurring on the property, such as criminal activity, fender-benders, or loud parties.

10. **Phone logs.** Document in a written log or computer file all incoming and outgoing business calls from residents, vendors or others relating to the rental business. Include the date, name, telephone number, substance of the conversation and time (especially if you are receiving harassing calls from residents). You cannot digitally record the conversations of others in California without their knowledge and consent.

POLICIES AND PROCEDURES OPERATING MANUAL

To ensure uniform practices by all employees, it is essential to have a written operating manual. Informative fair housing reminders should be inserted throughout each section to help staff realize how fair housing impacts virtually every action they take with their residents.

Even an owner/operator with a few rental units—or just one—should put his or her basic practices in writing. If the owner gets sick, goes on vacation or is otherwise unable to manage, whoever handles the property for the owner must know what to do.

If the temporary help discriminates in the owner's absence, the owner will pay the price.

Be sure to have the operating manual, whether in print form or stored as a computer file, reviewed for potential fair housing and landlord/tenant problems and suggestions.

For assistance creating or reviewing your policies and procedures operating manual, contact the KTS Fair Housing Practice Group at: KTSFairHousing@kts-law.com or (800) 338-6039.

Warning: **All** documentation should be professional, objective and non-discriminatory. Every shred of paper, computer record and file folder could end up being read by an investigator, a judge, a jury or the general public in court, a newspaper article or even more likely, somewhere on the internet!
◆

Domestic Violence

What is your policy when you find out a female applicant qualifies for your apartment in every way except for a domestic violence incident in her rental history? Do you refuse to rent to her? What if a current female resident is beaten up in her apartment by a boyfriend or spouse? What if the victim is a male? Do you promptly evict him or her or both of them? Do you have a zero tolerance policy in such cases? You may be surprised to know that these victims have many protections under fair housing law.

A 2001 case in Oregon and a Michigan case decided in 2003 regarding domestic violence may provide some clarity on this issue. The American Civil Liberties Union (ACLU), the National Organization for Women (NOW) and the U.S. Government participated in the Oregon lawsuit, and the ACLU filed the Michigan case.

Both cases raised the following arguments: Most domestic violence victims are women. Sex is a protected class under federal fair housing laws. Rental policies that result in a refusal to rent to anyone who has been involved in domestic violence have a tendency to affect more women than men (known as "disparate impact"). Accordingly, women are victimized twice, first by the perpetrator and then by management.

The VAWA
As a result of this and other similar situations, the Violence Against Women Act of 2005 (VAWA) became law. It was "renewed" in 2013.

It prohibits denial of admission or assistance under, termination from participation in, or eviction (under most circumstances) of victims of domestic violence, dating violence, sexual assault, and stalking from public housing, HUD subsidized- and mortgage-insured housing, the Section 8 Housing Voucher Assistance program, and the Low Income Housing Tax Credit Program. It provides assistance to victims of domestic violence, dating violence, sexual assault, and stalking who are also victims of severe forms of trafficking. Protection is extended "on the basis of actual or perceived race, color, religion, national origin, sex, gender identity (as defined in paragraph 249(c)(4) of title 18, U.S.C.), sexual orientation, or disability in persons."

On November 16, 2016, HUD published Final Rule 5720-F-03, updating the Code of Federal Regulations to implement the requirements of the VAWA. The Final Rule applies to "covered housing providers" which includes Section 8 project based and tenant based programs, as well as Section 202, Section 811, HOPWA, HOME, Homeless Programs, Section 221, Section 236, and the Housing Trust Fund. On June 30, 2017, HUD released Notice H 2017-05, providing additional guidance to owners and management agents with regard to the implementation of VAWA and HUD's Final Rule.

Pursuant to this rule, covered housing providers are required to provide applicants and tenants with "Notice of Occupancy Rights under the Violence Against Women Act" and certification forms during each of the following times: (1) upon denial of assistance or admission to the housing program; (2) upon admission to the housing program; (3) with any notification of eviction or termination of assistance; and (4) once during the 12-month period immediately following December 16, 2016 (the rules effective date).

The law also requires covered housing providers to develop and adopt an emergency transfer plan based on HUD's model emergency transfer plan.. The emergency transfer plan must outline a procedure which allows for the transfer of a victim of domestic violence, dating violence, sexual assault, or stalking upon request. Housing providers may, but are not required to, request specified documentation from a tenant seeking an emergency transfer under this rule.

A copy of HUD's final rule may be viewed at:
https://www.gpo.gov/fdsys/pkg/FR-2016-11-16/pdf/2016-25888.pdf

While HUD's Final Rule only explicitly applies to the "covered housing providers" as noted above, VAWA also covers the LIHTC and Rural Housing programs.

On January 18, 2017, the United States Department of Agriculture released Administrative Notice RD AN No. 4814 (1944-N) to provide direction to Rural Development (RD) Multi-Family Housing (MFH) programs affected by VAWA. A copy of the Adminstrative Notice may be viewed at: https://www.rd.usda.gov/files/an4814.pdf

On December 22, 2017, the California Tax Credit Allocation Committee (CTCAC) issued Low Income Housing Tax Credit ("LIHTC") Violence Against Women Act ("VAWA") Guidance to all property owners and management agents of LIHTC (Low Income Housing Tax Credit) properties to implement the Violence Against Women Reauthorization Act of 2013 (VAWA). A copy of CTCAC's memorandum and LIHTC Information and Checklist may be viewed at:

http://www.treasurer.ca.gov/ctcac/compliance/memos/vawa.pdf

California law

California law allows a resident who is a victim, whether male or female, (or whose household member is a victim) of domestic violence, stalking, sexual assault, elder abuse, dependent adult abuse or human trafficking to terminate tenancy by giving a 14-day notice and providing the landlord with a copy of a restraining order, protective order, police report, or documentation from a "qualified third party" indicating that the resident or household member is a victim of one of the protected acts. Documentation from a qualified third party must meet the following requirements.

- Documentation from a qualified third party based on information received by that third party while acting in his or her professional capacity to indicate that the resident or household member is seeking assistance for physical or mental injuries or abuse resulting from an act of domestic violence, sexual assault, stalking, human trafficking, elder abuse or dependent adult abuse.

- The "qualified third party" must be a physician and surgeon, osteopathic physician and surgeon, registered nurse, psychiatrist, psychologist, licensed clinical social worker, licensed marriage and family therapist or licensed professional clinical counselor. Alternatively, a sexual assault counselor, domestic violence counselor or human trafficking case worker can sign the documentation but only if the documentation displays the letterhead of the office, hospital, institution, center or organization that engages or employs the counselor or caseworker.

California law further prohibits (with certain exceptions) a landlord from terminating a tenancy based on one of the protected acts where the perpetrator is not a tenant and the victim has provided the landlord with a copy of a restraining order, protective order or police report alleging that the person is a victim of a protected act. Finally, the law prohibits a landlord from disclosing any information provided by a resident pursuant to Civil Code § 1946.7 to any third party unless:

(a) the resident consents in writing to the disclosure; or

(b) the disclosure is required by law or court order.

It is not considered to be a disclosure of information if the landlord communicates with a qualified third party who provided a statement that the resident was seeking assistance for physical or mental injuries or abuse resulting from a protected act for the purposes of verifying the contents of that statement. Note that victims in same sex relationships are also protected under the above law.

Termination of tenancy by the victim

The resident must notify the landlord that she (or a family member living in the same household) was a victim of domestic violence, sexual assault, stalking, elder or dependent adult abuse, or human trafficking and that the resident intends to terminate the tenancy. The resident must provide a written notice of termination to the landlord and must provide the landlord with a copy of one of the documents listed above. The victim must make his or her request to terminate the tenancy within 180 days of the date when the report was made or the order was issued by the court. The victim is responsible for the rent for 14 days after giving notice unless the unit is re-rented within that time period. The remaining resident(s) continue to be responsible for the rent.

Termination of tenancy by the landlord

California law prohibits a landlord from terminating a tenancy or refusing to renew a lease based on a protected act against a protected tenant or a protected tenant's household member unless the protected tenant has allowed the perpetrator back into the unit or the landlord reasonably believes that the perpetrator's presence poses a physical threat to others or poses a threat to a tenant's right to quiet enjoyment **and** the landlord has first given the protected tenant a 3-day notice to cure the violation before taking steps to terminate the tenancy.

Changing locks:
Civil Code Sections 1941.5 and 1941.6 further require a landlord to change the locks within 24 hours of a protected tenant's request when the perpetrator is not a tenant in the same unit and the tenant has provided the landlord with a copy of a restraining order against the perpetrator. The landlord must provide the protected tenant with a key to the new locks.

The landlord must also change the locks within 24 hours of a protected tenant's request when the perpetrator is a tenant in the same unit but the protected tenant has obtained a restraining order that excludes the perpetrator from the residence. Keys to the new locks must be provided to the protected tenant. In such an instance, the landlord cannot be held liable to the perpetrator for changing the locks and the perpetrator remains financially liable under any existing lease. If a landlord fails or refuses to change the locks under either of the above circumstances, the protected tenant has the right to change the locks and must provide the landlord with a key to the new lock.

You would be wise to check your current policies regarding domestic violence immediately and update them to reflect the current laws and fair housing viewpoint on this issue. ◆

Enforcement of Fair Housing Laws

F air housing laws are enforced at federal, state and local levels throughout the United States.

Federal: HUD
Federal fair housing laws are enforced primarily by the Department of Housing and Urban Development (HUD).

The Fair Housing and Equal Opportunity (FHEO) section within HUD is charged with enforcement. HUD has offices throughout the U.S. and investigates discrimination complaints nationwide regarding rental housing, real estate sales, insurance and lending, as well as any other businesses that impact housing.

- The statute of limitations for filing a complaint with HUD for an alleged violation is one year. (A statute of limitations prevents someone from filing a complaint if they wait too long.)

- In states with fair housing laws that are "substantially equivalent" with federal laws, such as in California, HUD complaints are generally referred to qualified state agencies for investigation.

Federal: Department of Justice

The Department of Justice (DOJ), led by the U.S. Attorney General, also enforces federal fair housing laws, the Americans with Disabilities Act (ADA) and civil rights laws. The DOJ often litigates "pattern or practice" complaints, in which an owner or management company implements policies or practices that routinely discriminate against applicants and residents (versus isolated incidents).

- The statute of limitations for filing with the DOJ is normally 18 months. Note that for some situations, the statute of limitations may be longer, particularly those cases involving non-compliance with the fair housing new construction accessibility requirements.

- Most of the DOJ cases come from HUD referrals.

State: DFEH

California fair housing laws are enforced primarily by the Department of Fair Employment and Housing (DFEH). It has offices throughout California and frequently investigates complaints on behalf of HUD since California laws are substantially equivalent to federal laws.

- The statute of limitations for filing a complaint with DFEH is one year.

- The DFEH, as of 1/1/2013, changed its structure and procedures. It replaced the Fair Employment and Housing Commission with a Fair Employment and Housing Council, giving it regulatory authority and ending administrative adjudication of fair housing claims. In short, it eliminated civil penalties, moving final adjudication to state court.

- If DFEH intends to pursue a discrimination case, it must do so by filing a civil lawsuit in Superior Court. Prior to DFEH filing a *fair housing* case, the parties are required to participate in *mandatory* dispute resolution, which is provided by a separate "wing" of DFEH.

- This means that when a case is not resolved and a lawsuit is filed in court, the cost of defending a discrimination case is dramatically increased. This is because the respondent (landlord) has to bear all of the costs and attorney's fees that are normally associated with civil litigation, including court filing fees, the costs of preparing and responding to discovery requests, deposition costs, expert witness fees, etc.

- If the DFEH prevails in a civil lawsuit, it has the right to seek to recover its attorney's fees and court costs However, you are not entitled to recover your attorney's fees from the DFEH even if you prevail.

The state attorney general's office also has the power to enforce state fair housing laws but does not commonly do so. The statute of limitations for the state attorney general is 18 months.

Local

Fair housing organizations throughout the state and country, such as councils or commissions, participate in enforcement in a variety of ways. They may provide such services as investigation, mediation, testing and referrals to administrative agencies or litigation in state or federal court.

Private attorneys

Persons who believe they have experienced discrimination may hire private fair housing attorneys, who must file suit in state or federal court. This right is *in addition* to the right to file with an administrative agency.

- The statute of limitations for a court filing is two years; however, under certain circumstances, it can be extended to three or more years.

- For example, if an incident occurred on 1/03/15 and a complaint was filed with DFEH 11 months later on 12/03/15 and, after another 11 months, it was determined that there was "no cause" or the complainant was unhappy with the progress of the case, the complainant could wait to file with an attorney in state or federal court as late as 2/03/16. This is because the court doesn't have to count the time during which the case was filed with the administrative agency. *(For more information, see the section on "Filing a Complaint.")*

Maintaining records

It is important to keep all applications (both accepted and denied), rental agreements and other documentation for a minimum of three, preferably four, years in case they are needed as evidence in a lawsuit. If your company is paperless, make sure you can produce hard copies of all original legal documents. There are stiff penalties for destroying or modifying such records after a complaint has been filed. ◆

Evictions and Fair Housing

It is not uncommon to have a resident who is being evicted raise the issue of discrimination. They may say "I am being evicted because we have children or because I have a disability (or make other claims that the manager is prejudiced against the particular group the person belongs to). In fact, the California Department of Fair Employment and Housing (DFEH) reported that approximately 20% of all complaints filed with DFEH are eviction-related. For this reason, it is essential to be both prepared for such an accusation and certain that the eviction is NOT discriminatory.

Under California law, you aren't required to state a reason for terminating a tenancy on a 30- or 60-day notice in a month-to-month situation unless it is necessary to be proactive in a defense against retaliatory eviction. Federal or local laws may require "cause" to be stated if a federal subsidy or an affordable program is involved, or the property is located in a jurisdiction that has a rent control or a "just-cause eviction" ordinance. Even when cause is not legally required on the notice, you should always have a non-retaliatory, non-discriminatory business reason for giving it—backed by good documentation.

If you are accused of having a discriminatory motive for an eviction, you will need one of two important types of evidence, preferably both, for a successful defense: *witnesses and documentation.*

First, witnesses can be invaluable. Unfortunately, most residents make reluctant witnesses—particularly if they fear retaliation by the resident you are evicting. In general, people don't want to get involved. It is helpful if you can get written testimony from the witness, but even that may be difficult.

Confirming letters: First, if a resident complains about another resident, ask for the complaint in writing.

If it is not forthcoming, you can write a confirming letter summing up the complaint as you understand it and send it to the complaining resident, stating that if you don't hear from him/her within a reasonable time period, (such as 10 working days), you will assume the facts expressed are correct. Then put a copy in the offending resident's file. It's not as good as something directly from the complaining resident, but it is better than an empty file. In lieu of a confirming letter, at the very least, document the complaint in the conversation log or as a memo in the resident's file.

Tell the resident who is alleged to have violated the rules about the problem and that further incidents could result in termination of tenancy. Then write a confirming letter regarding the substance of your conversation with the alleged problem resident. *(See the section on Complaints as well.)*

Documentation: Throughout the tenancy, document all resident contacts that may have legal implications. For example, make a record of an unusual number of repairs, noise complaints, excess foot traffic, threats of violence, harassment of neighbors or staff rules violations, unruly guests, police reports, etc. Make sure all documentation is professional, objective and non-discriminatory.

Remember that the lease covenants and house rules must be applied equally and consistently to all residents without regard to their status as a member of a protected class. If someone is violating rules, write a warning letter (according to your policy) and put a copy in the resident's file. If the behavior continues, serve the appropriate notice, place a copy in the resident's file and proceed with eviction if necessary. Develop a reputation for firm, fair enforcement of reasonable policies.

Rule out disability as a cause of the behavior
Many times, disruptive behavior or another failure to comply with the lease or rules is caused by a disability. Make it a habit to attempt to rule out potential disability *before* beginning the eviction process, keeping in mind that one cannot ask about a disability. If it can be shown that the behavior is the result of a disability, you may need to give the person an opportunity to come back into compliance. This means an eviction can be stopped dead in its tracks if a disability is alleged and an accommodation is requested (either directly or indirectly). If the behavior is a direct threat to the health and safety of the other residents, seek legal advice and proceed with caution.

Proving your case
The last thing you (or your attorney) want to happen is to get to court for an unlawful detainer and have the resident claim discrimination, only to find you have no evidence to prove otherwise. In the absence of supporting evidence, the court may very well decide in the resident's favor. Such a decision by the eviction trial judge could be used against you later in a fair housing complaint. ◆

Filing a Fair Housing Complaint

One of the most difficult and costly situations any owner or manager can experience is going through the fair housing complaint process. Even if you are doing everything by the book, you could still end up as a "respondent" in a fair housing lawsuit.

Who can file a complaint?

Anyone who believes he or she has been injured by an action or practice of a housing provider or someone associated with the provision of housing can file a fair housing complaint with an enforcing agency, private attorney or fair housing organization.

The California Fair Employment and Housing Act states, in Government Code §12955 (g), that an *"aggrieved person includes any person who claims to have been injured by a discriminatory housing practice or believes that the person will be injured by a discriminatory housing practice that is about to occur."*

In order to have "standing," or the right to sue, under California law, the complainant must be a member of the particular protected class at issue, or be *perceived* as being from that protected class or be *associated* with a member of that protected class. The complainant could be a resident, applicant, a tester on behalf of an administrative agency, a guest, an employee who is told by the employer to discriminate, a private fair housing organization or anyone acting on behalf of a person with a disability. In California, DFEH reports that about 15% of complaints are filed by applicants and about 80% of complainants are filed by in-place residents.

It is important to realize that discrimination is a painful and humiliating occurrence for those who experience it. Discrimination in housing can have life-altering consequences, such as denying a family the opportunity to live in a safe neighborhood with good schools for their children. Discrimination cases therefore can include penalties for emotional distress.

Filing the complaint

Complainants can be filed directly with any enforcing agency. They can file a complaint with HUD or DFEH:

- by completing a complaint or pre-complaint form on their websites,
- by using HUD's smart phone app,
- via telephone in a DFEH or HUD complaint or
- they can visit a nearby office in person.

(See the "Enforcement of Fair Housing" section.) Many of the procedures noted in this section are also appropriate to a suit filed in court by a private fair housing attorney without involvement of government enforcing agencies.

Who can be named in the complaint?
In 2016, HUD updated the Code of Federal Regulations to clarify who may be liable for discriminatory housing practices. HUD defines two types of liability: direct liability and vicarious liability. CFR §100.7, states:

(a) *Direct liability. "(1) A person is directly liable for: (i) the person's own conduct that results in a discriminatory housing practice. (ii) Failing to take prompt action to correct and end a discriminatory housing practice by that person's employee or agent, where the person knew or should have known of the discriminatory conduct. (iii) Failing to take prompt action to correct and end a discriminatory housing practice by a third-party, where the person knew or should have known of the discriminatory conduct and had the power to correct it.*

(b) *Vicarious liability. A person is vicariously liable for a discriminatory housing practice by the person's agent or employee, regardless of whether the person knew or should have known of the conduct that resulted in a discriminatory housing practice, consistent with agency law.*

As a practical matter, this means that the name of the alleged perpetrator and everyone up the chain of command will normally be named in a fair housing complaint. This includes anyone in authority who has control over the alleged perpetrator. For example, if the leasing agent is the alleged violator, then the community manager, property supervisor, owner of the management company and owners of the property may be named.

Some of the other entities with fair housing liability include appraisers, architects, builders, advertising agencies, newspaper publishers, real estate agents and brokers, lenders and insurance companies.

If the complaint is ignored by management
Never ignore a complaint. If you do, you will be in default, which can be very costly.

You will be better off either defending your position or settling (particularly if it appears you may have discriminated or if there is no way to prove you didn't). And if you wait until the day before the response deadline before deciding to seek legal assistance, you've made the attorney's job of defending you much more difficult.

Once you find out a complaint has been filed

Contact your attorney—one who is experienced in handling fair housing cases. If you do *anything* wrong at this point, it can cost you and your company a huge, unnecessary expense. In other words, rarely is this a do-it-yourself situation. Owners or managers can say the wrong things, get overly defensive or make other missteps that can damage their cases. With the restructured DFEH, you could even find yourself in a court of law, paying attorney fees to the state of California.

Our attorneys have already established good working relationships with the administrative agencies and can handle your case quickly and effectively.

Again, NEVER ignore a complaint. It needs to be handled promptly. The longer the case drags on, the worse your chances will be for a successful resolution.

Contact your insurance company. The owner and/or management company should determine whether or not you have specific coverage for fair housing. If in doubt, contact your agent. If you are covered and decide to make a claim, let the company know promptly. A delay could invalidate your claim. The company may provide you with an attorney or cover your costs with your existing attorney. Note that if there is a finding of intentional discrimination, your insurance may not provide you with any coverage.

Gather the facts.

1) Find out whom in your company or on the property knows about the situation addressed in the complaint;

2) Gather as much information and documentation as possible;

3) Put together a chronology of events regarding the situation.

Select a point person to be responsible for all contact with your attorney (or administrative agency if you elect not to use an attorney).

The California complaint process

Most HUD complaints filed against California properties are referred to the DFEH for investigation. DFEH must serve notice on the respondent (owner/manager) and at this point, serves as a neutral, fact-finding agency.

Normally, HUD or DFEH notifies management in writing that a complaint has been filed and requests a response or answer within 20 days. Mediation is required. If there is no resolution, they will investigate the complaint to determine if there is reasonable cause to believe there has been a fair housing violation. They have the authority to request a variety of documents and information as part of the investigation. If necessary, they can subpoena the information. DFEH is also required to attempt a conciliation between the parties.

Conciliation

In a conciliation, HUD or DFEH will try to reach an agreement with the parties. Any conciliation agreement must protect both the complainant and the public interest. If an agreement is signed, HUD or DFEH will take no further action on the complaint. If HUD or DFEH has reasonable cause to believe that a conciliation agreement has been breached later, the agencies will recommend that the state or federal attorney general file suit against the party that has breached the agreement.

If reasonable cause is determined

If the agency finds reasonable cause to believe that discrimination occurred, it will let you know. For HUD cases, it should be heard in an administrative hearing within 120 days unless either party wants the case to be heard in Federal district court. If so, the complainant will be provided with an attorney at no charge. During the period prior to the hearing, the complainant can still hire a private attorney and bring suit in state or federal court.

Pursuant to the 2013 restructure of DFEH, if the agency finds cause to believe that discrimination has occurred, it must now bring a lawsuit in Superior court as DFEH no longer has the ability to conduct an administrative hearing.

In some instances, HUD or DFEH may reach a finding of "no cause" and decline from pursuing any further action. However, keep in mind that even in cases in which there has been a finding of "no cause," the complainant can still hire a private attorney and bring suit in state or federal court.

However, the case is usually weakened by the finding of "no cause" by the administrative agency

The length of time the case has been with the agency normally does not count towards the two-year statute of limitations for a court action. In a lawsuit filed in a state or federal court with a private attorney, if the case does not settle prior to trial, it will be heard in a court trial before a judge and/or jury. ◆

Harassment

On September 14, 2016, issued Final Rule 63054: Quid Pro Quo and Hostile Environment Harassment and Liability for Discriminatory Housing Practices Under the Fair Housing Act. This final rule amends HUD's fair housing regulations to formalize standards for use in investigations and adjudications involving allegations of harassment by providing for uniform treatment of Fair Housing Act claims raising allegations of quid pro quo and hostile environment harassment in judicial and administrative forums. This rule applies to all housing providers (conventional and subsidized).

This final rule provides definitions of two specific types of harassment, quid pro quo ("this for that") and hostile environment, and specifies how HUD will evaluate complaints of these types of harassment under the Fair Housing Act. While previously applied most commonly to sexual harassment claims, HUD's new rule applies to harassment claims on the basis of race, color, religion, national origin, sex, familial status, or disability. A copy of this Final Rule may be found at:

https://www.gpo.gov/fdsys/pkg/FR-2016-09-14/pdf/2016-21868.pdf

Immigration Issues

Illegal immigration has been at the forefront of the news for the last several years. In the past, a number of cities throughout the country enacted local ordinances penalizing landlords if they rented to someone who is determined to be in the country illegally.

Most of these ordinances are not in effect because of court decisions declaring them illegal or unconstitutional.

The California legislature then passed a law prohibiting local governments from passing any law that would compel a landlord (or a landlord's agent) to inquire into, disclose or report upon or provide any information regarding an applicant's citizenship status.

The law also prohibits local governments from requiring that landlords or their agents refuse to rent to a person or discontinue renting to a person because of his/her citizenship status.

Finally, the law prohibits landlords or their agents from inquiring about citizenship or immigration status or requiring that an applicant or current resident provide any information about his/her citizenship or immigration status.

In 2015, the California Legislature again refocused its efforts to protect the rights of all persons, by passing SB 600, which added "citizenship" and "immigration status" (as well as "primary language") as protected classes within the Unruh Act. The Legislature made it a point to clarify that the addition of these protections is declaratory of existing law.

In 2017, the California Legislature passed Bills AB 291 and AB 299, known as the Immigrant Tenant Protection Act, creating several protections intended to prohibit housing discrimination or harassment based on immigration or citizenship status.

Civil Code §1940.05 defines immigration or citizenship status to include a person's actual immigration or citizenship status, as well as a perception that a person has a particular immigration or citizenship status, or that a person is associated with a person who has, or is perceived to have, a particular immigration or citizenship status.

Civil Code §1940.2 was amended to prohibit a landlord from threatening to disclose information regarding or relating to the immigration or citizenship status of a tenant, occupant, or other person associated with a tenant or occupant of a dwelling, for the purpose of influencing a tenant to vacate a dwelling.

Civil Code §1940.3 was amended to prohibit a landlord from inquiring about or disclosing to any person or entity information regarding or relating to the immigration or citizenship status of any tenant, prospective tenant, occupant, or prospective occupant of the rental property for the purpose of, or with the intent to, harass, intimidate, retaliate, or influence a tenant to vacate a unit.

New Civil Code §1940.35 prohibits landlords from disclosing information regarding the immigration or citizenship status of a tenant, occupant, or person associated with the tenant, to any immigration authority, law enforcement agency, or local, state, or federal agency, for the purpose of, or with the intent of, harassing or intimidating a tenant or occupant, retaliating against a tenant or occupant for the exercise of his or her rights, influencing a tenant or occupant to vacate a dwelling, or recovering possession of the dwelling, irrespective of whether the tenant or occupant currently resides in the dwelling. The law does allow such disclosure to comply with any legal obligation under federal law, including, but not limited to, any legal obligation under any federal government program that provides for rent limitations or rental assistance to a qualified tenant, or a subpoena, warrant, or other order issued by a court.

Code of Civil Procedure §1161.4 will prohibit unlawful detainers based on immigration or citizenship status unless the landlord is complying with a federal affordable housing program. Code of Civil Procedure §1161.4 also will affect a landlord's ability to request a social security number, consumer credit report, or identification, if the landlord has already approved the tenant to take possession of the unit.

The new law also adds Civil Code § 1940.05 (defining "immigration or citizenship status), modifies Civil Code §1942.5 (regarding landlord retaliation against tenants), Business & Professions Code §6103.7 (attorney discipline), and adds Civil Code §3339.10 (to specify that immigration and citizenship status are irrelevant in most landlord tenant disputes).

As a practical matter, this means that your rental applications should not ask any questions about citizenship or immigration status. Your rental criteria should not require an applicant to be a citizen or a legal immigrant. The law does, however, allow a landlord to continue to require information or documentation necessary to determine or verify an applicant's financial qualifications and/or identity or to comply with federal law (such as HUD-subsidized housing program requirements).

Fair housing advocates and enforcing agencies have long been of the opinion that determining a person's legal status should be left to the federal government (which regulates immigration) and not have it be the responsibility of private property owners. It can be very difficult (even for immigration officials) to determine whether a person is in the country legally. And unlike employment laws, there currently are no federal laws or regulations that have been interpreted to require or allow that penalties be imposed on a landlord for renting to an undocumented immigrant.

The only situation in which there is a stated responsibility to check immigration or citizenship status is in project-based HUD-subsidized housing through a special government program called "SAVE." ◆

Insurance for Fair Housing

Defending against a fair housing complaint can be very costly. Not only are there business expenses associated with providing documents and witnesses, there are court costs and attorney fees, whether you are found guilty or not. If you are found to have intentionally discriminated, your insurance is not likely to provide any coverage. If it was unintentional, you may still end up paying a hefty settlement, fine or award and bearing the expense of mandatory training and other follow-up requirements.

Most standard property insurance packages do not cover fair housing. However, it is often available at an additional cost. All property management companies and all rental property owners should make sure they have this coverage. If your agent says that you are covered, insist on written verification of the coverage. Employees should check to see if they are covered by their company's insurance. If not, they may want to obtain their own policy. The California Apartment Association currently offers several types of discrimination insurance policies for its members at www.caanet.org.

Keep in mind that no insurance will cover willful or intentional discrimination or other illegal acts. If a lawsuit is brought by a fair housing attorney, he or she may claim that management was *negligent* in the situation, for example, negligent hiring or negligent supervision. Technically, this could be a good thing for you because it normally triggers your standard insurance for negligence. However, this may not be the case if a complaint is filed with an administrative agency.

Potential Expenses

- A HUD Administrative Law Judge can award civil penalties ranging from up to $19,787 per occurrence for a first offense, $49, 467 for a second offense and $98,935 per occurrence for repeat offenses.

- The Department of Justice (DOJ) has assessed civil penalties as high as $200,000 and can also assess punitive damages.

- Punitive damages, which are unlimited, can be awarded in either an administrative proceeding or a court case and can range from a few thousand to a few million dollars.

- There can be compensatory damages, injunctive and equitable relief.

- The federal court or federal administrative law judge (or in California, the Superior Court) may award damages for embarrassment, humiliation, emotional distress and unlimited punitive damages.

- Don't forget the cost of attorney fees (including the complainant's attorney's fees if you lose the case), depositions, expert witnesses and filing fees, as well as the administrative costs of preparing for the investigation and hearing or trial.

Often, due to concerns of the potential large damage awards and the ever-increasing costs of litigation, many fair housing cases often settle rather than go to trial. However, even cases that settle can involve significant monetary payments, in addition to other penalties.

Recent cases include:

- On November 29, 2017, DFEH announced a $100,000 settlement involving a San Jose landlord alleged to have discriminated against tenants with disabilities by refusing to allow them to have emotional support animals.

- In October 2017, HUD announced a conciliation agreement between the Fair Housing Advocates of Northern California (a fair housing organization) and a Marin County landlord. In the underlying complaint, the owners/managers were alleged to have discriminated against a female tenant with disabilities who required an assistive animal. As part of the conciliation agreement, the owners/management will pay over $70,000.

- In October 2017, DFEH reached a settlement with a Bakersfield landlord and property Management Company with regard to occupancy limits. In the underlying complaint, the landlord and management company are alleged to have discriminated against families with children by applying restrictive occupancy standards. Specifically, they are alleged to have denied a 12 person household the opportunity to rent a 2,583 square-foot home because the family had "too many kids" and applying a two-plus-one occupancy standard.

- In May 2017, HUD settled a discrimination complaint HUD announced a $20,000 settlement with the owner and manager of a Mountain View, California apartment complex.

In the underlying complaint, the owner and manager are accused to have discriminated against residents based on their national origin and familial status. The manager is alleged to have repeatedly stated that he did not like have Latino tenants at the property, prohibited children from playing at the property, and terminated the lease of a Latino household after their two (2) year old daughter was heard crying loudly.

- On November 17, 2016, DFEH settled a housing discrimination case against a San Francisco Landlord for $575,000. In the underlying action, the resident, who had lived in the property for over 50 years, made disability-related accommodation requests to the landlord to allow her to have a live-in caregiver, have the landlord accept checks signed by her sister, and provide her with a more accessible entrance to the property's trash room. The landlord is alleged to have denied her reasonable accommodation requests, refused to accept her rental payments, and served her with multiple eviction notices.

- On 9, 2016, DFEH announced a $75,000 settlement involving a Los Angeles Landlord and an 85-year old disabled tenant. In the underlying action, the landlord allegedly denied the tenant's repeated requests to be transferred from the second floor to a first floor apartment (the property does not have an elevator) after she began using a wheelchair after developing Parkinson's disease and experiencing multiple strokes and heart attacks.

- In July 2016, the owners and manager of an apartment complex in Lakewood, Colorado settled a familial status lawsuit for $75,000. In the underlying action, the manager was alleged to have told prospective renters that families with children were generally placed in the rear building of the property and adults (without children) in the front. As part of the settlement, the owners must also receive fair housing training, establish new nondiscrimination policies and application and rental procedures, and conduct monitoring and reporting to HUD for a 3-year period. ◆

Investigations

When a fair housing complaint is filed with an administrative agency, the agency will normally conduct an investigation to help determine if there has been a violation. The investigation may include the use of testers *(see the section on "Testing" for more information).* The agency may require that management submit certain documentation, interview residents or employees or use other methods as necessary. If a complaint is being filed in state or federal court by a private attorney, the information will normally be obtained by subpoena. The amount of information requested can be staggering.

An experienced fair housing defense attorney can guide you through the investigative process and, if necessary, help facilitate the documentation submissions. He or she can often narrow the scope of the investigation, which can save you time and money.

Documents

Initially, the agency (or attorney) will send the owner a list of documents that it would like to review. If the information is not voluntarily provided, the government agency has the power to subpoena the information—which doesn't necessarily start the investigative experience off on very good footing. (Note, however, that no information should be turned over to an agency or complainant's attorney without a subpoena or formal discovery request and approval from your own attorney.)

The requested information may vary, depending on the type of complaint. A complaint by a current resident might require information regarding community policies, maintenance records, eviction files or other documents that could demonstrate the type of treatment residents receive during their tenancies.

A "refusal to rent" complaint would primarily entail information regarding your leasing and screening process. Information that management may be required to provide can include the following:

- Names and addresses of all owners of the property in question and a list of all other properties owned;

- Names, titles and addresses of all management personnel, plus a list of all properties managed;

- All advertising during that past year;

- Denied applications for the past 12 months, plus reasons for each denial;

- Applications and leases/agreements of all new residents during the past 12 months;

- Policies and procedures regarding rental criteria, written screening procedures, maintenance records, community policies, advertisements, etc., and

- Evidence of fair housing training for the employee being accused of discrimination. (For this reason, a sign-in sheet should always be used at all trainings and kept for three, preferably four years.)

  - This also includes certificates of completion or other evidence that an employee has successfully completed an online fair housing training.

You can see why it is essential to have a thorough documentation program in place and to be sure that it is being implemented on a daily basis by all personnel. It is recommended that all records be kept at least three years, preferably four, which is the statute of limitations for the breach of a written contract, in case a state or federal lawsuit is filed several years down the line. Lack of documentation can prevent you from proving there was no discrimination.

If there was discrimination and you are tempted to "lose" harmful documentation, be advised that there is a separate $100,000 penalty for interference with or destruction of evidence. Under Federal law:

Sec. 811. [42 U.S.C. 3611] (c) Criminal Penalties.
(1) Any person who willfully fails or neglects to attend and testify or to answer any lawful inquiry or to produce records, documents, or other evidence, if it is in such person's power to do so, in obedience to the subpoena or other lawful order under subsection (a), shall be fined not more than $100,000 or imprisoned not more than one year, or both.
(2) Any person who, with intent thereby to mislead another person in any proceeding under this title--
(A) makes or causes to be made any false entry or statement of fact in any report, account, record, or other document produced pursuant to subpoena or other lawful order under subsection (a);
(B) willfully neglects or fails to make or to cause to be made full, true, and correct entries in such reports, accounts, records, or other documents; or

(C) willfully mutilates, alters, or by any other means falsifies any documentary evidence; shall be fined not more than $100,000 or imprisoned not more than one year, or both.

Other residents may also be interviewed by investigators to see if they have had experiences similar to those alleged by the complainant.

Discussions by staff are discoverable

Remember that all discussions between staff members about applicants and residents must be kept professional and non-discriminatory at all times. Such discussions are discoverable in a court of law—meaning they can be revealed in an investigation, deposition or publicly before a judge or hearing officer. If there are offensive comments being made, it can indicate to the investigator that there is a negative environment and attitude at that property toward members of certain protected classes.

To illustrate this point, there was a California case not long ago, in which two onsite personnel had been overheard by a resident from a protected class discussing the fact that they disliked persons from that particular protected class and wanted to keep them out of the property. The resident filed suit and prevailed after an investigation found racial discrimination on the property.

Reminder: *Contact an attorney first when faced with a complaint.* ◆

Laws Regulating Fair Housing

air housing laws include federal, state and local ordinances. On many issues, state and federal law are very similar, and in some sections, they are identical. However, since states have different population profiles and different environments, many states have enacted additional laws—or more stringent versions of the federal requirements. Local municipalities also face some unique situations, and some have enacted still more laws to meet the needs of their local residents. These state or local laws may only add to, not dilute, diminish or take away, the fair housing rights given by the federal government.

FEDERAL LAWS

The key federal fair housing laws that managers and owners of rental property should be familiar with include the following:

The Civil Rights Act of 1866. This Act became law immediately after the Civil War. It is found in *Title 42, The Public Health and Welfare, Chapter 21, Civil Rights, Subchapter I.*

> *Section 1982. All citizens of the United States shall have the same right, in every State and Territory, as is enjoyed by white citizens thereof to inherit, purchase, lease, sell, hold, and convey real and personal property.*

This was the first time citizens other than white citizens had property rights and is still cited in certain complaints based on race when there is intentional discrimination. Over the years, race has been held by the U.S. Supreme Court to cover some forms of ethnic or religious discrimination, such as the Irish, Arabs and Jews.

The Civil Rights Act of 1968, Title 8. This Act, which was ratified six days after Dr. Martin Luther King Jr's assassination, was the result of many years of struggle by the civil rights movement. Today, when we talk about the federal Fair Housing Act (FHA)—this is it! The FHA is codified in the *U.S. Code, Chapter 45, Sections 3601 through 3631.* It set forth four protected classes: race, color, religion and national origin. It was amended in 1974 to include sex as a protected class.

The Fair Housing Amendments Act of 1988. The Fair Housing Act received a major overhaul when the Federal Fair Housing Amendments Act (FHAA) was enacted during the Reagan Administration in 1988. It added two protected classes (familial status and handicap) and greatly increased the administrative enforcement powers.

The Code of Federal Regulations. The Regulations, or "Regs," which have been established by HUD (following public input), are used to define and carry out the fair housing laws. They provide more extensive implementation details than the Fair Housing Act itself. These regulations have the full force and effect of law and are found at 24 CFR Part 100, et. seq.

CALIFORNIA LAWS

California's fair housing laws are "substantially equivalent" to the federal laws; however, additional requirements have been placed on owners and managers of rental property by the state legislature and court decisions.

The Fair Employment and Housing Act. Originally called the Rumford Act (1963), the Fair Employment and Housing Act (1980), or FEHA, was made equivalent with the federal Fair Housing Act effective January 1, 1994. Half of the Act refers to discrimination in employment; the other half covers "for sale or rental" housing. The state has incrementally added several protected classes to those covered by the federal Fair Housing. The first were marital status, sexual orientation, ancestry and source of income. It was expanded in 2004 to include "gender identity" for transgendered persons under the definition of "sex." In January 2012, gender, gender identity, gender expression and genetic information were added to the FEHA as separate areas of protection. The Government Code currently reads:

> *§12955. It shall be unlawful:*
>
> *(a) For the owner of any housing accommodation to discriminate against or harass any person because of the race, color, religion, sex, gender, gender identity, gender expression, sexual orientation, marital status, national origin, ancestry, familial status, source of income, disability or genetic information of that person.*

The FEHA also voids any covenants or rules that forbid or restrict the use/sale, etc. of real property because of a person's protected class. For example, at one time, when a person bought a home in a particular development, the covenants restricted who could live there . . . generally allowing only white residents. The only non-white persons who were allowed to live there were servants. Some older developments may still include such covenants, and, even though they are not enforced, they are still illegal and must be removed.

The Unruh Civil Rights Act. This Act pertains to discrimination in business, which includes the sale and rental of housing. Although found in the Civil Codes, it is considered to be incorporated into the FEHA above. This Act adds "age" and "medical condition" to the protected classes, as well as a catch-all called "arbitrary discrimination" (discriminating against a person or group of persons based on personal characteristics). The Unruh Act itself does not use the words "arbitrary discrimination;" however, several decisions by the California Supreme Court have used the terminology, including in 1982 when the Court concluded in *Wolfson v. Marina Point,* that refusing to rent to families with children was "arbitrary" and therefore discriminatory.

Effective January 1, 2006, the Unruh Act included sex, race, color, religion, ancestry, national origin, disability, medical condition, marital status and sexual orientation as protected classes "in all business establishments in California of every kind whatsoever."

In 2012 a new definition of "sex" was added to the Unruh Act.

> *(5) "Sex" includes, but is not limited to, pregnancy, childbirth or medical conditions related to pregnancy or childbirth. "Sex" also includes, but is not limited to, a person's gender. "Gender" means sex, and includes a person's gender identity and gender expression. "Gender expression" means a person's gender-related appearance and behavior whether or not stereotypically associated with the person's assigned sex at birth.*

As of January 1, 2016, three new protections were added: citizenship, primary language and immigration status. Section 51 of the *Civil Code* has been amended to read:

> *(b) All persons within the jurisdiction of this state are free and equal, and no matter what their sex, race, color, religion, ancestry, national origin, disability, medical condition, genetic information, marital status, sexual orientation, citizenship, primary language, or immigration status are entitled to the full and equal accommodations, advantages, facilities, privileges, or services in all business establishments of every kind whatsoever.*

The Act also states that it is a violation to discriminate based on a "perception" that the person has any particular characteristic or characteristics within the listed categories or that the person is "associated" with a person who has, or is perceived to have, any particular characteristic or characteristics within the listed categories.

An example of perception (or perhaps better stated "misperception") would be if you told an applicant who you thought was gay that no apartments were available (when apartments were in fact available), but the applicant was not actually gay.

An example of association would be if a white applicant brought someone from another race along while apartment hunting and you told the applicant nothing was available (when it actually was) because the applicant's friend was from a different race. Note that there are numerous complaints filed in California that are based on association.

The Act also provides extensive requirements for senior housing in California, which are more stringent and detailed than federal law.

The California Disabled Person's Act. This Act is also found in Section 54 of the Civil Code, following the Unruh Act above. It states *that "Individuals with disabilities shall be entitled to full and equal access, as other members of the general public, to all housing accommodations offered for rent, lease, or compensation."* It also covers accommodations, modifications, access to transportation and service dogs.

LOCAL ORDINANCES

Local municipalities can adopt additional fair housing requirements as long as those requirements provide greater protections than state or federal laws. For example, San Francisco and Santa Cruz have added "size" (height and weight) to the protected classes; Berkeley has added "students" to its protected classes. Check with your local apartment or real estate organization, which may know if there are additional ordinances in your community. ◆

Limited English Proficiency (LEP)

On September 15, 2016, HUD released new Guidance on Fair Housing Protections for people with Limited English Proficiency (LEP). Not to be confused with HUD's LEP rule which applies only to federally funded housing and requires owners and operators of federally funded housing to provide translation services under certain circumstances this new Guidance applies to ALL housing.

In this Guidance, HUD discusses the correlation between language barriers and national origin discrimination as applied to housing. HUD concludes that, "where a policy or practice that restricts access to housing on the basis of LEP has a discriminatory effect based on national origin, race, or other protected characteristic, such policy or practice violates the act if it is not necessary to serve a substantial, legitimate, nondiscriminatory interest of the housing provider, or if such interest could be served by another practice that has a less discriminatory effect."

As a practical matter, the HUD Guidance suggests that if low cost translation services are available, a landlord should provide them. Moreover, HUD indicates that compliance with a state law would not be an excuse to refuse to provide translation services to someone with limited English proficiency. This could create challenges for California landlords, as under California Civil Code §1632, if a California residential lease primarily negotiated in Spanish, Chinese, Tagalog, Vietnamese or Korean, the lease must be provided to the tenant in that language.

As this Guidance raises risk management decisions on the part of owners and management, it is strongly recommended that any new policies being considered by reviewed by an attorney with expertise in fair housing before implementation. ◆

Maintenance

Both maintenance practices and maintenance personnel can be the subjects of a fair housing complaint. Your maintenance team, including landscapers, porters and other support personnel, is a very important part of the overall management team and has considerable exposure to residents. *(For more detailed information on the impact of fair housing on maintenance, please see our special publication, "The California Maintenance Fair Housing Guide," which is in both English and Spanish.)*

- Have written procedures for handling maintenance requests from residents to ensure that all residents receive fair and equal treatment.

- Make sure your on-line or printed work order form requests detailed information from the resident about the problem and contains space for information about the work done and follow-up information.

- Be sure to let residents know what you consider to be an emergency so there are no misunderstandings when you attend to an emergency request before an earlier request that was not time-sensitive.
  The needs of a resident with a disability may change a normal repair to emergency status. For example, a clogged toilet in a second bathroom is normally not an emergency unless that second bathroom is the only accessible bathroom for use by a resident who uses a wheelchair.

- Do not enter a resident's apartment to make a repair if there is a minor (under the age of 18) present but no adult. Reschedule to a time when an adult will be present. If it is an emergency that needs immediate attention, take someone with you if possible.

- Do not enter the apartment of a resident who is inappropriately dressed. Explain that you will be back at a more convenient time, return to the office and document the situation.

- Don't discuss residents with other residents. If a resident asks you about another resident, such as about someone's disability or marital status, let the resident know that you never discuss private information about other residents.

- Don't agree to make impromptu repairs for residents unless your company policy allows it. They should make their requests to the office in accordance with your normal procedure or someone might claim that you are giving preferential service.

- No ethnic or dirty jokes or stories and no sexual comments ever. ◆

Occupancy Standards

Occupancy standards is one of the most controversial areas of fair housing law, partly because:

a) some owners and managers feel it is their property and they can establish whatever rules they want,

b) there is still a reluctance to rent to families with children (even though it has been required in California for over thirty years) and

c) currently, there are no specific federal or state laws regarding minimum occupancy, only guidelines used by enforcing agencies as triggers for familial status complaints. Federally, two persons per bedroom is generally accepted, but not without many exceptions.

Note that there may be minimum occupancy requirements in project–based subsidized properties to ensure the maximum use of each unit.

Historically, many properties have used occupancy limits as a tool to prevent families with children from living there. In 1982, the California Supreme Court ruled in *Wolfson v. Marina Point* that it was "arbitrary discrimination" based on the Unruh Civil Rights Act to refuse to rent or sell property to families because they had children. Marina Point was an adult property that attempted to force the Wolfsons to move because they had given birth to a baby.

After the ruling, many owners and managers reduced their occupancy standards to one person per bedroom as a method of skirting the decision. Others already had long-established limitations that were similar but which had the same effect on families. Many properties were constructed as adults-only communities and had to face angry adult residents who didn't want children living nearby. Landlords were not sure how to react.

Ultimately, the Department of Fair Employment and Housing established an occupancy guideline in an attempt to assure a more reasonable opportunity for families to find housing.

The California guideline of *two persons per bedroom plus one for the unit* is followed in most cases. Some owners have established a guideline of two persons per bedroom *plus two for the unit* to make sure they don't have a problem. (Note: there may be other occupancy requirements in some project-based HUD-subsidized programs.)

Is the guideline a guaranteed safe harbor? No, because there can be configurations or conditions in some properties that could merit either more or fewer occupants. For example, a large single-family home with a family room and two large bedrooms might easily accommodate more than five persons. By way of example, in October 2017, DFEH reached a settlement with a Bakersfield landlord and property Management Company with regard to occupancy limits. In the underlying complaint, the landlord and management company are alleged to have discriminated against families with children by applying restrictive occupancy standards. Specifically, they are alleged to have denied a 12 person household the opportunity to rent a 2,583 square-foot home because the family had "too many kids" and applying its two-plus-one occupancy standard. According to the DFEH press release, as part of the settlement, the management company agreed to "end the use of any occupancy standard that has the effect of discriminating against families with children".

On the other hand, a tiny studio or SRO (single room occupancy), which could be considered a one bedroom for occupancy purposes, might be unsuitable for three persons. For these small spaces, the formula outlined in the Uniform Housing Code (which is based on square footage that could reasonably be used for sleeping) is normally applied. There can also be other considerations, such as septic tank limitations, that might make the guideline unworkable for a given property.

The occupancy standard you establish for your property should be backed by a supportable, non-discriminatory business reason.

In some areas, local ordinance or building or health and safety code standards may be used to determine occupancy limits. In those laws, the maximum number of people permitted is usually based on the square footage of the potential sleeping areas of the dwelling.

An example is the City of San Francisco, which has an ordinance making it unlawful to refuse to rent to a family with children due to the number of occupants, as long as that number does not exceed the maximums established by the local Housing Code (which are higher than the state guideline). The ordinance also states that children under six cannot be counted when determining the size of the household. ◆

Phone Calls and Phone Logs

The potential for violating a fair housing law begins with the first contact with an applicant, which is often a phone call. In fact, many discrimination cases involve phone calls—who said what to whom and when they did it. Therefore, never underestimate the <u>importance of a good phone log, current rental information and good training.</u>

Phone logs

You should document *all incoming and outgoing business calls.* Written spiral bound carbon copy phone logs were previously the preferable method as courts were skeptical of computer records because they could be altered or created after the fact. However, phone logs today are most often created and retained via computer. Over time, courts and enforcing agencies have become more accepting of computer records as valid evidence, although some companies continue to maintain written chronological phone log records (such as a spiral bound notebook).

Regardless of what method you use, include such information as a) date; b) time; c) name of person, if you can get it, otherwise "male" or "female" will suffice; d) what the person wanted or called about; e) what you said and f) your name or initials.

This information is invaluable to refresh one's memory or to defend a case if the person who made the notes is no longer at the property. And you'll find there are many other important uses for your phone logs—for marketing, maintenance requests, harassing calls, complaints, etc. Keep your phone logs for a minimum of three, preferably four, years.

Timely, accurate information

Make sure you have the most *current* rental/vacancy information next to the phone or readily available on your computer to ensure that you are giving all callers the same accurate and timely information. If an apartment has already been rented by someone on your team, you need to know about it now before you've made an appointment with someone to come see it. You need to tell everyone the same rental and security deposit amount, the same availability date, the same number of bedrooms and the same features for the same vacant dwelling.

Linguistic profiling

Linguistic profiling has become a fair housing issue in recent years. It involves forming opinions about applicants based on their accents or the sound of their voices and making rental decisions based on those opinions.

If applicants who "sound" foreign or as though they are from a particular race are treated differently, they may rightly assume that they have experienced discrimination. A suspicious applicant has only to ask a friend without an accent or from a different race to call about the vacancy to quickly determine whether it is likely that discrimination has just taken place.

Beginning in 2016, SB 600 added "primary language" (as well as "citizenship" and "immigration status") to the enumerated protections within the Unruh Act. The Legislature made it a point to clarify that the addition of these protections are not to be considered new protected classes, but rather is declaratory of existing law.

Linguistic profiling easily extends to voice mail or answering machine messages. A subtle discriminatory approach sometimes used by management may be to either "forget" to return the call or unnecessarily delay the callback. Be sure you have a written policy for returning calls from persons who leave messages on your voice mail—then follow it and document that you did so in your phone log.

Testing for linguistic profiling continues to be conducted nationwide. In a well-publicized follow-up report on phone testing for treatment of Hurricane Katrina victims in five states, 66% of the black callers experienced discrimination. Negative treatment included not having calls returned; being given less information; and being quoted higher rents, security deposits and income requirements, as well as not being offered special incentives that were offered to white callers. The testing results were turned over to HUD for investigation and litigation.

Name profiling

In a related form of profiling, some managers and owners form opinions over the phone based on the *name* of the caller. Many groups are identifiable by their names. For example, race and/or national origin can commonly be determined because of a name's unique characteristics. Your impressions should never enter into your decision to call back or rent to a potential applicant. Follow your written policies for phone calls, email and online inquiries with all callers.

Discriminatory questions

- Don't ask, "Do you have any children? How old are they? Are those your children I hear in the background?" (Note that some federally-subsidized housing programs may require such information, which may be considered an exception to the general rule.)

If you have a *bona fide* senior property, simply indicate the age restrictions up front to all prospective residents.

- Don't ask, "And are you a single person? What is your relationship to the other applicants?"

- Don't ask, "I notice you are kind of shaky, do you have Parkinson's or something?" "I can't identify your accent...are you from somewhere in the Middle East?" "I hope you don't mind me asking but are you and your partner gay?" None of those things are relevant to whether or not an applicant will be a responsible resident.

  (If your property is subsidized and has a program for persons with disabilities or accessible units, you may be required to find out if applicants qualify for them.)

- Don't ask, "Where do you work? Do you have a job somewhere?" Such questions may make the applicant think s/he must be employed to be considered for tenancy. Additionally, it forces applicants with disabilities who cannot work to disclose that information to you.

  Let applicants provide income information on the application since you cannot discriminate based on source of income in California. You can't require someone to be employed.

If a shopping agency is hired to evaluate the manager and leasing personnel, make sure the service doesn't require that your employees ask questions that are discriminatory in order to receive a good evaluation score. If they do, find another agency immediately. Some agencies are national in scope, so their questions may be acceptable in other states but not California.

- Do ask questions relevant to tenancy selection that are appropriate to ask.

- With regard to your website rental applications, questions that shouldn't be asked in person or on in-office applications should also not be a part of any internet applications. Some companies advertising on the internet may be national in scope, but questions that are appropriate in other states may not be appropriate for properties located in California.

Ask the same questions of all applicants
Have a standard list of non-discriminatory questions that you normally ask every caller who is interested in your property.

For example, you can ask such question as

- The caller's name,
- When the unit is needed,
- How many bedrooms/baths they want,
- What amenities they are interested in ,
- Do they prefer a certain location, such as upstairs or down and/or
- How many persons will be living in the unit. ◆

Photo IDs

Fair housing laws do not allow you to collect information, or make "verbal or written inquiry," about a person's sex, nationality, race, color, etc. Therefore, we recommend that you avoid making photocopies of an applicant's ID (which discloses much of that information) and attaching it to the application. It's not worth the fair housing risk. Additionally, it would be hard to prove that your rental decisions were not influenced by information shown on the photo IDs. Fair housing advocates have stated that if they see photo IDs attached to applications, it will be used against management. It is the timing of the photocopying that makes the difference.

Using the photo ID when giving a property tour
For safety purposes, when doing personal tours of the property, many managers request that a photo ID of at least one person in the party be left in the office. The ID or photocopy should be placed in a locked drawer to avoid identity theft. Although it is recommended that you NOT make a copy, if you do, return the copy to the applicant when you return from the tour or shred it in the person's presence. In California, when businesses dispose of sensitive paperwork, they are required to shred all personal information that might be used in identity theft. For more security, use a cross-cut shredder. Never just toss the photocopy into the trash.

Matching the information on the photo ID
When the applicant submits an application, by all means, take a long, hard look at the photo ID. Learn some of the signs of a fake ID. Take the time to see if the picture matches the face of the applicant and that the date of birth appears to match the applicant's age. Is the address on the ID listed on the application? If not, ask why not. Make a notation of the additional address. Check to see that the name is the same. Is it spelled the same?

If the name on the ID is a full name and the name on the application is a nickname, note the difference. You won't get an accurate credit report if you don't have an accurate name.

Attaching a photo to the signed rental agreement for the files
After the applicant has been approved as a resident, you can attach a copy of the photo ID to the rental agreement or lease. While even this practice may have some privacy concerns, you have several good business reasons for having each resident's ID in the file. For example, you don't want to let someone into an apartment who claims to be locked out if he or she isn't a permitted occupant. Note: Do not make a copy of a military ID. It is illegal to copy military IDs under Title 18, U.S. Code Part I, Chapter 33, Section 701. ◆

Posters, Fair Housing

Federal fair housing law requires that every property of <u>four or more units</u> have a federal fair housing poster displayed in a conspicuous location. It should be displayed in the rental office or place of business where it will be seen by applicants when they apply for an apartment or by residents who come to do business in the office. It must state:

U.S. Department of Housing and Urban Development

EQUAL HOUSING
OPPORTUNITY

We Do Business in Accordance With the Federal Fair Housing Law
(The Fair Housing Amendments Act of 1988)

> **It is Illegal to Discriminate Against Any Person**
> **Because of Race, Color, Religion, Sex,**
> **Handicap, Familial Status, or National Origin**

- In the sale or rental of housing or residential lots
- In advertising the sale or rental of housing
- In the financing of housing
- In the provision of real estate brokerage services
- In the appraisal of housing
- Blockbusting is also illegal

Anyone who feels he or she has been discriminated against may file a complaint of housing discrimination:
1-800-669-9777 (Toll Free)
1-800-927-9275 (TDD)

U.S. Department of Housing and Urban Development, Assistant Secretary for Fair Housing and Equal Opportunity, Washington, DC 20410

Specifically, the regulations state, *"All fair housing posters shall be prominently displayed so as to be readily apparent to all persons seeking housing accommodations or seeking to engage in residential real estate-*

---

related transactions or brokerage services as contemplated by sections 804 through 806 of the Act."

Size requirements

Reducing the size of the poster to 8½ by 11 inches violates the size requirements specified by law. Part 110 of the federal Regulations says, *"The fair housing poster shall be <u>11 inches by 14 inches</u>."* As a practical matter, it is difficult to read a smaller size type from across the room; therefore, we recommend that you follow the requirement. It defeats the purpose of the poster when it isn't in a readable size and is also out of compliance.

Obtaining a federal poster

The supply is often spotty. You can try your local apartment association, local fair housing council or the nearest HUD office.

A free federal fair housing poster is also available from HUD on the internet at:
https://www.hud.gov/sites/documents/FAIR_HOUSING_POSTER_ENG.PDF
(both English and Spanish versions are available from their website). You'll have to enlarge it to the required 11 x 14 inches, however. You can also order them from companies who offer them for sale, but be sure to order the correct size. Don't forget to frame it attractively!

Obtaining a California poster

The California Fair Housing poster is available at the website of the Department of Fair Employment and Housing (www.dfeh.ca.gov). While not required by law to be posted, DFEH prefers that you do so. The federal poster lists only the federal protected classes while the DFEH poster includes the additional California protected classes.

There are two versions of the current poster, a two page version, and a one page condensed version, making it easier to post.. You could also have it laminated and readily available in the leasing office or provide a copy with your promotional materials when an applicant enters the office.

The purpose of these posters is 1) to inform applicants about their fair housing rights by providing resources and telephone numbers to call if they have a question or complaint and 2) to demonstrate the owner's or management company's intention to abide by fair housing laws. In a fair housing investigation, the presence or absence of the federal poster (and in some cases the California poster) will be noted. The absence of the federal poster is considered to be a *per se* violation of the Fair Housing Act. ◆

Pro-Active Fair Housing Measures

What does an applicant experience when he or she comes to your property? Imagine you are an applicant from a protected class entering your office. Look around. Is there *anything* visible to indicate that the manager of this property will be welcoming and give you an equal opportunity to live here? If there isn't, would you wonder if this is going to be another one of those "experiences" where you are told, "Sorry, we don't have any vacancies right now"?

But what if instead, you walk into a rental office to apply and see a fair housing poster properly displayed on the wall and a nicely framed company fair housing policy displayed on the wall beside the poster? Would you be more likely to feel that you may have an equal opportunity to live at this property? Add a brochure printed with the fair housing logo and the property's activity binder or iPad promotion with pictures of happy residents enjoying themselves—residents of all kinds— and you just may think, "I'm home!" *Which scenario does **your** property present to applicants?*

Demonstrating fair housing compliance
There are certain key items that that can indicate a company's commitment (or possible lack thereof in their absence) to providing equal housing opportunity to *all* persons. They include the following:

Fair housing policy statement
The owner or management company should have a written, company-wide fair housing policy statement that expresses the intention and commitment to comply with all state, federal and local fair housing laws. It should point out that employees who discriminate may be subject to termination of employment.

This policy statement should be read and initialed by every employee and placed in his or her file. Some companies also display their policy statement, or a summary of the statement, on the rental office wall along with the name and phone number of a supervisor whom an applicant or resident can call if the person believes he or she has not been treated fairly.

Poster *(See the previous section on "Posters")*
The federal Fair Housing Poster must be prominently displayed at every property with four or more units. The regulations state that it must be 11 x 14 inches. Frame it if you wish. You are also encouraged to display the California Fair Housing Poster.

Logo

Use the fair housing logo liberally: on your business card, letterhead, brochures and flyers, forms—everywhere. Use the logo in display ads, in rental publications or newspapers and on your website.

Operational policies and procedures manual

Note that an operations policies and procedures manual is NOT the same thing as an Employee Manual. This company "how to" manual tells employees, step-by-step, how to handle each aspect of operating the property.

It is an important tool even if you are an owner/operator with one or two units. It helps you establish consistent practices to be followed by you and anyone else assisting you with the operations and/or management of your property. If you are sick or on vacation, whoever fills in for you needs to know what to do so you don't come back to a fair housing complaint! If you have employees, you should include a special fair housing section in your policies and procedures manual that covers the basic requirements.

Have your policies and procedures manual reviewed periodically by a knowledgeable fair housing attorney who is able to recognize any potential fair housing problems. Laws change, court decisions vary and there are frequently new interpretations of old issues.

Fair Housing Knowledge

Everyone who is involved in any aspect of management should attend at least one three-hour fair housing class each year. There is SO much to learn that no one can assimilate it all in one sitting. Even those of us who specialize in fair housing education are constantly learning new things—finding out about new interpretations, new guidelines, new court rulings and new nuances in old laws. Investigators of a discrimination complaint almost always ask if owners or staff have had training and what that training was. It helps if you have a student outline with notes that you have taken during classes and a certificate of completion. This includes online courses you might take as well. Generally, a three-hour course is the acceptable standard, which is also required for a compliance training. In other words, a one-hour class isn't enough time to provide adequate information. If there has been no recent training, an investigator may easily assume discrimination has occurred.

- Start a fair housing file folder on your computer. Keep records showing that you have been making a diligent effort to learn how to comply with fair housing laws. Keep your notes and handouts from seminars, as well as certificates of completion (which you may need later to prove attendance). *Even some employers are asking job applicants if they have had fair housing training in the past!* If you see an article in a magazine or newspaper about a recent fair housing decision or case, add it to your file.

- Periodically check the internet for <u>current</u> fair housing information. See the Resources section in the Appendix of this book for useful websites that provide fair housing laws and timely information.

- When you see something of interest, add it to your ever-growing file folder. Always keep in mind that information from federal sources or other states may not be entirely accurate for use in California.

- And lastly, read and reread this Encyclopedia from cover to cover and obtain an updated version each year. ◆

Properties Covered / Partially Exempted by Fair Housing Laws

In California, ALL housing that is for sale or rent is covered by fair housing laws. Federal laws have a number of exclusions, but since not all the exclusions are applicable in California, and to avoid confusion, they are not included in this Encyclopedia. Housing that is covered includes apartments, condos, single family homes, marinas, mobile home parks, travel trailer parks, retirement homes, shelters, time shares and more.

In California, the following types of housing *have partial* exemptions from portions of the law:

Senior housing (55 and over or 62 and over)
In order to have *bona fide* senior housing, a number of state and federal requirements must be met. They are defined in the Unruh Civil Rights Act, found in the California Civil Code, Sections 51–53. Federal law sets forth a number of requirements for validating that the housing is, indeed, senior housing. This type of housing may exclude children under most circumstances. However, senior housing may not discriminate against the other protected classes such as race, color or nationality.

Religious or membership organizations
Religious groups may show a preference for their followers in housing that is owned or operated for non-commercial purposes (such as housing for nuns or priests or faith-based residential recovery homes). Other groups (such as fraternities) may require that one be a member in order to qualify to live in their housing. Operators of such housing are still prohibited, however, from discriminating against any other protected classes such as race, color or nationality.

One roomer or boarder
Both California and federal law provide that "owners" (which includes tenants in possession) may rent to ONE roomer or boarder who lives *within* the household, sharing living facilities such as kitchens, bathrooms, living room, etc., and such "owners" may select whomever they wish.[4] They may advertise a preference for a male or female roommate but may not mention any other protected class limitations in their advertisement or subsequent discussions with applicants. This exception is only for ONE roomer. If there are TWO or more roomers, all fair housing rules apply and male or female preferences may not be mentioned at all.

Additionally, if the person has a private entrance and the room or rooms being rented are locked off from the rest of the house, it is considered to be an apartment situation and does not qualify for the exemption.

One reason this exception was made was as an accommodation for the elderly. For example, an elderly woman living alone who needs to rent out a room for financial reasons may not feel comfortable renting to a male who would be sharing her kitchen, living room or bathroom.

Colleges and universities
In California, institutions of higher education may provide housing reserved especially for students, families with children, males, females or married students/domestic partners. Again, they may not discriminate against any other protected classes such as race, color or nationality.

Private student housing is not exempt
Currently, *private* owners and management companies who operate student housing in the state of California are doing so at their own risk.

---

4. A tenant would need permission of the owner to sublet to an additional occupant per the lease. If permission is denied, the proposed additional occupant would need to apply and be screened like other residents.

In some instances, owners or operators have been given a variance from a city to provide school-related housing. Unfortunately, the city's endorsement is not likely to protect the owner/operator if it is determined that there is a violation of state law. If, however, management operates university or college-owned properties on behalf of the school, they *may* be covered by the exemption.

California Government Code Section 12995 states, *"(a) Nothing contained in this part relating to discrimination in housing shall be construed to: (2) Prohibit any postsecondary educational institution, whether private or public, from providing housing accommodations reserved for either male or female students so long as no individual person is denied equal access to housing accommodations, or from providing separate housing accommodations reserved primarily for married students or for students with minor dependents who reside with them."*

There is an argument that operating privately-owned student housing pursuant to a contract with a college or university should be considered to be exempt, but in general, showing a preference for students in private housing is likely to result in a claim of discrimination on the basis of age, source of income, marital status, familial status and arbitrary discrimination. ◆

Protected Classes

There are groups of people living within our society that have historically and statistically received unfavorable treatment with regard to housing. They have been denied housing, charged higher loan rates, been prevented from buying real property, given different terms, charged higher rents or security deposits or experienced a lower level of service during their tenancy than other groups of people.

Equal opportunity, not special rights
The intention of federal and state fair housing laws is to require that ALL persons, regardless of protected class status, be given *equal treatment and the same services* and offered an equal opportunity to live in housing of their choice—in other words, the *same rights as everyone else.* The only exception to this is for persons with handicaps (federal term) or persons with disabilities (California term) who have been given several special rights in order to achieve equal opportunity.

Federal protected classes

At the federal level, there are currently seven classifications:

- **Race:** This was the first protected class, established right after the Civil War in 1866. It is the second most common basis of complaint when coupled with "color." They are combined because it is difficult to determine whether the violation occurred because of the person's race or color.

- **Color:** There can be many shades of skin color within each race. Further, many people are a blend of multiple races. Often the color of a person's skin is what is first noticed, not the person's race. Persons with darker skin often experience more incidents of discrimination in housing, as well as in other day-to-day situations.

- **Religion:** Religion is an emotional subject for many people. However, we should not base our housing decisions on what religion a person does or doesn't follow.

  In 2013, FEHA's definition of "religious creed" was amended to explicitly include "religious dress practice" and "religious grooming practice." "Religious dress practice" includes the wearing or carrying of religious clothing, head or face coverings, jewelry, artifacts, and any other item that is part of the observance by an individual of his or her religious creed, while "religious grooming practice" includes all forms of head, facial and body hair that are part of the observance by an individual of his or her religious belief. The law specifically states that the terms "religious dress" and "grooming practices" should be broadly construed. This applies primarily to the employees of the company.

  Also, employers are expected to accommodate the employee and try to find reasonable alternatives to any rules or work duties that conflict with their religious beliefs, to the extent that the accommodation does not constitute an undue hardship. There are special concerns for employers in property management because it has long been held that religious dress could mistakenly be assumed to indicate that an employee would show preferences in housing decisions based on religion. Seek legal advice before addressing this subject with employees.

  An accommodation is not considered reasonable if it requires segregation of the individual from other employees or the public.

- **Sex:** Discrimination based on one's gender is prohibited. Sexual harassment is also covered under this protected class, and there are an increasing number of cases alleging harassment.

  - o In 2003, California redefined "sex" to include "gender identity" in the Fair Employment and Housing Act in California. Therefore, transgender persons should receive the same treatment and opportunities as everyone else.

  - o In 2012, California clarified that discrimination is not allowed under state law on the basis of gender-related appearance or expression, whether or not stereotypically associated with a person's assigned sex at birth. Gender, gender identity and gender expression are now listed as California protected classes.

  - o Current California law includes gender, pregnancy, childbirth and medical conditions relating to pregnancy and childbirth in the definition of the protected class of "sex." The definition has been expanded to include "breastfeeding or medical conditions related to breastfeeding" in the Fair Employment and Housing Act.

- **National origin:** This category protects persons who have come from other countries. Illegal immigration in housing is a hot topic throughout the country today, but inquiries into one's citizenship or immigration status is illegal in California.

  - o As of 1/1/2016, there are new California protections based on immigration status, citizenship and primary language. While these are not separate protected classes, the new law requires that they must receive the same quality of services in all businesses.

  - o In 2016, HUD released guidance discussing the correlation between language barriers and national origin discrimination as it applies to housing. (*For more information, see the section on limited English proficiency (LEP)*)

- **Familial status:** Any household that includes persons under the age of 18 is protected under familial status. Pregnancy is also included in this category. Only *bona fide* senior housing can exclude children.

- **Handicap** (called "**disability**" in California): California's definition of disability is considerably broader than the federal law, covering certain medical conditions as well as mental and physical impairments. It does not require that the disability "substantially" limit a person's ability to perform a major life activity, as in the federal law. A pamphlet from DFEH defines it as "an impairment that makes performance of a major life activity 'difficult'." Unlike federal law, California law extends the definition to include persons whose impairment is lessened or eliminated by the use of devices such as eyeglasses.

  The two special rights extended to persons with disabilities include 1) the right to make reasonable modifications to a dwelling to enable them to live there comfortably and 2) the responsibility of management to make reasonable accommodations in rules, practices, policies and services in order to allow persons with a disability to fully enjoy their tenancy. *(See "Reasonable Modifications" and "Reasonable Accommodations.")*

California Protected Classes

The FEHA, as of January 1, 2014, includes the following bases for discrimination in housing:

> "... any person because of the race, color, religion, sex, gender, gender identity, gender expression, sexual orientation, marital status, national origin, ancestry, familial status, source of income, disability, or genetic information of that person."

The California Unruh Civil Rights Act, which prohibits discrimination in business, which includes the sale and rental of housing, states:

> "All persons within the jurisdiction of this state are free and equal, and no matter what their sex, race, color, religion, ancestry, national origin, disability, medical condition, genetic information, marital status, sexual orientation, citizenship, primary language, or immigration status are entitled to the full and equal accommodations, advantages, facilities, privileges, or services in all business establishments of every kind whatsoever."

- **Marital status:** The marital status of applicants and residents is irrelevant to the rental of housing. Don't ask about or make a decision based on a person's marital status. (Note: some project-based HUD-subsidized housing programs may require that applicants list the "relationship" of the proposed occupants or ask for a person to be designated as "head of household.")

- **Sexual orientation:** This covers persons who are heterosexual, homosexual or bisexual. Don't ask about a person's orientation or lifestyle or make rental decisions based on their orientation.

- **Age:** The Unruh Act specifies "age" as a protected class. Therefore, avoid making rental decisions based on age, such as not wanting to rent to the elderly or young persons. (The only exception is *bona fide* senior housing, which must adhere to strict age guidelines. *For more information on these limits, see the section "Senior Housing."*)

- **Ancestry:** Going beyond national origin, rental decisions should not be based on someone's ancestry. This often includes name profiling, wherein the landlord avoids renting to someone whose last name appears to be "foreign" even if the person's family may have been in the U.S. for many generations.

- **Source of income**: Don't require or imply that applicants should be employed in order to qualify to rent. Their income or financial resources only need to be legal and verifiable—and of an adequate amount to meet your established rent-to-income ratio. Section 8 vouchers are not currently considered a source of income under state law. (*See the section on "Section 8 - Tenant-based Housing Choice Voucher Program"*).

  o In January 1, 2014, military status was added to the FEHA employment protected classes, but it hasn't yet been included in the housing classifications. Nevertheless, it could be relevant since source of income discrimination is protected with regard to housing.

- **Medical condition:** Although this was originally an employment issue (some employers didn't want to hire persons with cancer or who were genetically predisposed for certain diseases in order to avoid higher insurance costs), it is now clearly protected in housing situations.

- **Sex: The Unruh Act has redefined "sex," in California to include:**

  (5) "Sex" includes, but is not limited to, pregnancy, childbirth or medical conditions related to pregnancy or childbirth. "Sex" also includes, but is not limited to, a person's gender.

- **Gender: The Unruh Act then defines "Gender" as:** *"sex, and includes a person's gender identity and gender expression.*

  - *Gender expression means a person's gender-related appearance and behavior whether or not stereotypically associated with the person's assigned sex at birth."*

- **Genetic information: The Unruh Act defines "genetic information" as:** *"Genetic information" means, with respect to any individual, information about any of the following:*

  I. *The individual's genetic tests.*

  II. *The genetic tests of family members of the individual.*

  III. *The manifestation of a disease or disorder in family members of the individual.*

- **Citizenship, Primary Language, and Immigration Status:** Effective January 1, 2016, the Unruh Civil Rights Act was amended to add citizenship, primary language, and immigration status as protected classes within the Unruh Act, and is applicable to all businesses throughout the state (including rental housing). The Legislature made it a point to clarify that the addition of these protections is declaratory of existing law.

Other Protections:

- **Arbitrary discrimination:** *California* also covers "arbitrary discrimination," which means discriminating against a person or group of persons based on their personal characteristics, such as persons who wear dreadlocks or have multiple tattoos.

- **Perception and Association:** California is usually on the cutting edge of legal issues. Two unique concepts have been added to state law, which are not protected classes. They pertain to protected classes and can be used as a basis for an allegation of discrimination: perception and association.

- o *Perception:* If someone is treated unfairly because he or she is mistakenly perceived to be a member of a particular protected class, the unfair treatment is considered an act of discrimination even if it was based on a misperception.

- o *Association:* Discriminating against someone because his or her friends or guests are from a particular protected class is also a violation.

Other states

Other states have added protections for additional groups such as military status, Section 8, or students.

Local protected classes

In fact, many counties and municipalities across the country have addition al protected classes, making compliance challenging. In San Francisco, for example, height and weight have been added. It joins Santa Cruz, Washington, DC, and Michigan, which have similar laws prohibiting discrimination based on body size. Berkeley has added "students" as a protected class.

Which groups experience the most discrimination?

Throughout California and the U.S., the largest number of discrimination cases is based on disability (over 50%). Race/color is the second, and familial status is the third most common basis. ◆

Rental Criteria
Non-Discriminatory Eligibility Standards

There are important reasons why you should have your rental criteria carefully thought out and put into writing.

- It helps assure that all your residents meet your qualifications.

- It helps ensure that all applicants are being treated equally and consistently.

- Applicants who have received written criteria up front and who do not meet those standards are more likely to bypass applying (and wasting their application fee money) or are less likely to file a complaint if rejected.

- If there is a fair housing complaint based on refusal to rent, you will be required to provide your written criteria as part of the investigation.

There is no standard list of qualifications that should apply to all properties. Standards tend to vary by location, by type of property, by the typical resident profile, etc. Over time, you will also learn how much risk you are willing to take with applicants' qualifications. Make sure the standards do not impact anyone unfairly and that you have supportable, non-discriminatory business reasons for establishing each one. And finally, make sure your qualifications are in writing and are given to each applicant early in the interview process.

Please refer to our legal workbook, "Establishing Your Rental Criteria," for more detailed assistance, available for order at www.kts-law.com. It is designed to assist you in developing or modifying your qualifications and avoid fair housing risks.

The following are some of the rental qualifications you may want to consider for your property:

Occupancy standards

Set a reasonable occupancy standard that is appropriate for your property. Be able to back up your standard with a reasonable, non-discriminatory business reason. There is no "safe harbor" number that you can rely on.

California's historical guideline for triggering a familial status complaint is generally anything less than *two persons per bedroom plus one* for the unit. However, cases have been filed despite adherence to these guidelines, particularly if a property has large rooms and could reasonably accommodate more people. Also, some cities, such as San Francisco have passed ordinances that require landlords to allow a higher occupancy than the state guideline.

Second-tier or "conditionally-accepted" applicants

- *Adverse Action.* If you have a second tier of qualifications for those who don't meet your fully qualified standards, put that criteria in writing and apply it to everyone. Applicants who are not automatically disqualified because of something such as a recent eviction or current bankruptcy would then have an opportunity to rent if they meet your additional requirements, such as an increased security deposit or a having a cosigner.

Technically, these applicants are being denied residency unless they can meet your second tier qualifications. Therefore, you must fulfill your adverse action responsibilities according to the federal FCRA (Fair Credit Reporting Act) and FACTA (Fair and Accurate Credit Transactions Act). Refer to the KTS Residential Preventive Law Handbook for specific information on the requirements of these Acts.

- *Co-signers/Guarantors.* If you permit co-signers for less-than-fully qualified applicants, you must permit them for everyone in a similar situation. You should require the co-signer to fully meet your financial standards (or meet a higher standard since the co-signer must be able to pay the tenant's rent in the event of a default as well as his/her own rent or mortgage payment).

    Most companies evaluate only the financial/credit qualifications of the co-signers since the person will not be living on the property or be named on the lease. The co-signer should sign a separate guarantor agreement rather than signing the lease, otherwise they may be argued to have tenancy rights with regard to the unit.

(See the important article on the 2003 court decision regarding co-signer policies and accommodations in the Appendix.)

Source of income

In California, you cannot require that applicants be employed nor show a preference based on the source of their income. Don't establish requirements that could exclude fully qualified people who might be retired, self-employed, receive government benefits or assistance, etc., who can demonstrate financial responsibility. You may assure yourself of that financial responsibility by checking to see that the source of income is legal and verifiable. You may also establish reasonable rent-to-income ratios for your property. Section 8 vouchers are not currently considered a source of income under state law; however, several counties and cities have passed local ordinances identifying Section 8 vouchers and other rental assistance programs as protected sources of income. (*See the section on "Section 8 - Tenant-based Housing Choice Voucher Program"*).

Don't show source of income preferences (a violation of California law) by giving discounts to medical or law enforcement personnel or nearby employers (Preferred Employer Programs), for example. Offering military discounts could even be considered a preference based on income source.

Criminal records

Be cautious about using convictions, arrests or other criminal records in your criteria. The FHA states that convictions for the "manufacture and distribution of illegal, controlled substances" can be the basis for denial of an application. The FHA further states that you do not have to rent to a person who is a *current, direct threat* to the health and safety of your residents or the property.

Accordingly, if you are going to deny an application for a conviction that is outside the scope of manufacture or distribution of a controlled substance, you must be prepared to defend that denial on the basis that the person's *past* conviction makes them a *current* direct threat and will prevent them from being a responsible resident. *(Note: Project-based HUD-subsidized housing programs may include a requirement prohibiting you from renting to persons convicted of certain crimes.)* In 2016, HUD issued new Guidance for all housing providers regarding how the use of criminal background checks could potentially violate fair housing laws. *(See the section on criminal background checks).* It is strongly recommended that decisions regarding criminal background policies and the individual assessments required by the HUD Guidance in this area be made by owners or upper management rather than by on-site employees. It is also recommended and that the policies be reviewed by an attorney with expertise in fair housing in light of the HUD Guidance.

Social security numbers

It is common practice to request a social security number (SSN) in order to run a credit report. Some individuals, particularly those from other countries, may not yet have one or may not need one. It is important to remember that there is no law requiring a person to obtain a social security number in order to live in the U.S. unless they are employed. Therefore, to ensure that all applicants have an equal opportunity to obtain housing, you should have an alternate means of running a credit report for those applicants without social security numbers. Even if your screening company tells you they can't do it without a SSN, there are companies who can and will run them using information such as the applicant's name, Individual Taxpayer Identification Number (ITIN), date of birth and last known address. The main drawback is that you may not get a good match between the information and the person as you would with a screening that uses a social security number.

(Most project-based HUD-subsidized programs require that social security numbers be provided for all members of the household from six years of age and up or provide a certification stating that the family member has never received a social security number.)

Photo IDs/Immigration status

Proof of identity for all adults is important. You may require government-issued photo identification but don't require that the ID be a driver's license since not everyone drives. In 2015, the DMV began issuing driver's licenses to undocumented immigrants. These licenses contain an identifying mark indicating that the person has not provided proof of citizenship to obtain the license. Our caution is that management should not use the driver's license to deny housing because the law specifically states you cannot discriminate on the basis that someone holds this type of license.

As of 2016, "citizenship" and "immigration status" (as well as "primary language") were added to the protected classes within the Unruh Act, which applies to all businesses (including rental housing) throughout the state. The Legislature made it a point to clarify that the addition of these protections are not to be considered new protected classes, but rather is meant to be declaratory of existing law. Additionally, under Civil Code Section 1940.3, you may not make any inquiry about an applicant's or resident's citizenship or immigration status.

Don't require that the ID be a U.S. or state-issued ID, as that may exclude persons from other countries (national origin discrimination). Further, requiring a U.S. or state-issued ID would likely violate California law, which, as mentioned above, prohibits landlords from inquiring about the person's citizenship or immigration status.

Compare the information on the government-issued ID to the application information and the photo to the applicant. Note any differences. *(For more information on the use of photocopies of IDs, please refer to the section on Photo IDs.)*

Protected classes

In conventional housing, don't establish criteria that makes reference to age, children, familial status, disability, race, skin color, religion, national origin or ancestry, marital status, sex, sexual orientation, source of income, medical condition, gender, gender identity, gender expression, primary language, citizenship, or immigration status, or any other arbitrary discrimination based on the personal characteristics of the applicant, such as body shape or size, clothing choices, body decorations, etc.

(Note that some project-based HUD subsidy programs require age, citizenship or immigration status, relationship and other such information.)

Financial standards

You can establish financial standards to help ensure that the applicant is going to be monetarily responsible, such as setting a rent-to-income ratio and specific credit requirements.

Rent-to-income ratio: Based on your property, its location and typical resident financial profile, determine a reasonable ratio that will reduce your risk of non-payment of rent. For example, to qualify, an applicant must have a gross income of two (or 2.5 or 3) times the monthly rent.

Lack of employment: If the person is not employed but has other income or funds available, have reasonable standards that accommodate such circumstances. For example, you might require a person to show he or she has six months' rent and reasonable living expenses available in a bank account if he is requesting a six-month lease, or ask for proof of income via tax returns for a self-employed applicant. Because of potential eviction complications, we do not recommend requiring rent to be pre-paid.

Credit worthiness: Many owners' sole requirement is "good credit" or "positive credit." What does that mean? Be specific so you can apply the same standards to every applicant. Can the person have charge-offs? Accounts in collection? If so, how many are acceptable? How many negatives are acceptable? How many late payments? Will you accept someone who has had a bankruptcy in the past year? Three years? What about outstanding medical debts? Or a recent foreclosure? These are all things to consider and to address in your criteria. It is important to be reasonable. For example, what if a bankruptcy, eviction, foreclosure or charge-off occurred six or seven years ago but the person has shown financial responsibility since then?

In lieu of a social security number for a credit check, if unavailable, some properties have started to ask the applicant to bring in evidence of financial responsibility, such as six months' worth of proof of payment of rent, utility bills and other similar verification of financial responsibility.

Rental and eviction history

You want residents who have a good rental history. That means they have paid their rent on time, taken good care of previous rental homes, been good neighbors and have not caused waste or created a nuisance. In short, you want to rent to those who have been responsible residents in the past.

If you rely solely on credit checks to determine if an applicant will be a good resident, remember that many problem residents have good credit and have never been evicted. Checking on rental history can avoid many future problems. They may pay the rent on time but create problems on the property and then move before an eviction can be filed. Unless there is a money judgment in an eviction, it will not be reflected in a credit report.

Contacting former landlords for rental histories should be done appropriately, only asking questions about issues relating to the fulfillment of the lease. *(A list of potential questions can be found in the Appendix.)* If this is your practice, make sure you check rental histories for every applicant, not just for those you may not want to rent to.

If you do check rental history, it is important to have specific standards in writing that can be applied consistently among all applicants. Will you accept persons with eviction records? What if the eviction was five years ago and the person has been a responsible resident since then? What if the person has not been evicted, but has caused other problems at the property?

Note that if an applicant's rental or eviction history includes past negative behavior caused by a disability, and now steps have been taken to resolve those issues, and if the applicant otherwise qualifies, you may need to give that person an equal opportunity to be considered as a resident. Denying housing based on the disability could be considered a fair housing violation. If you have a question about an applicant with this background, consult with your attorney for guidance.

Update your criteria regularly

Be alert to changing trends in the market, and test your standards frequently. For example, if you have a standard that requires an applicant to have lived at his present address continuously for the past six months or a year and the applicant is a high-tech employee newly recruited from a foreign country by a local company (and would otherwise qualify), would your standards accommodate that person if he otherwise qualified? Could there be discrimination based on national origin? An annual review is critical since you may not be aware of new laws and interpretations. ◆

Rental Terms and Conditions

All applicants must be offered the same rental terms and conditions for the same dwelling. (However, there can be an exception if a co-signer or larger security deposit would be required for a "conditionally accepted" applicant who otherwise would not qualify.)

The Federal Fair Housing Act specifically states that it is illegal *"To discriminate against any person in the terms, conditions, or privileges of sale or rental of a dwelling..."*

The Federal Regulations are even more succinct. *Sec. 100.65* adds further definitions of instances of discrimination: *(1) Using different provisions in leases or contracts of sale, such as those relating to rental charges, security deposits and the terms of a lease and those relating to down payment and closing requirements, because of race, color, religion, sex, handicap, familial status, or national origin.* In California, you must also include age, ancestry, sexual orientation, gender, gender expression gender identity, marital status, medical condition, genetic information and source of income as additional protected classes. Equal treatment must also be extended based on immigration status, primary language and citizenship.

In California, approximately 25% of all complaints are based on unequal terms and access to facilities. Therefore, check your policies to make sure that, unless the exception applies for conditionally accepted applicants, you are:

- Offering the same rent and security deposits for the same unit to all applicants (see exception above);

- Offering the same lease period to everyone rather than a month-to-month agreement for families and a one-year lease to adult households, for example (with a possible exception of a short, provisional month-to-month term for a conditionally-accepted applicant);
- Offering the same opportunities for payment of rent or security deposits;
- Offering "rent specials" to everyone when such specials are available, not just those who ask about it;
- Offering a wait list to all applicants, if you have one when no apartments are currently available that meet the applicants' needs; and
- Offering the same opportunities for use of the property (including families with children).

Negotiating rents
Beware of negotiating rental rates with a prospective resident in order to close a deal (or in order to retain a current resident). If you do not offer that same lowered rental rate or opportunity to negotiate equally to all prospects or current residents, you could be opening yourself up to a potential claim of discrimination.

If a prospective or current resident could prove that the policy of negotiating leases has a disparate impact on one or more protected classes, that policy could be deemed discriminatory.

For instance, it might be alleged that certain groups of people are less likely to ask whether the price can be negotiated, such as single mothers (protected by the classes of marital status, familial status and/or gender) or persons from certain cultures (which could be a race and/or national origin/ancestry issue). A policy that is found to have a disparate impact will be considered non-discriminatory unless 1) there is a legitimate business necessity behind the policy and 2) it can be shown there is no less discriminatory way to accomplish that legitimate business necessity.

In the context of negotiating deals to fill apartments or retain current residents, a business necessity might be shown through vacancy logs and financials for the property. In order to show there was no less discriminatory way to accomplish the business necessity, a property may need to show what other marketing/retention methods have been tried without success.◆

The Screening Process

Screening is one of the most important steps in the leasing process for several reasons. If it is done poorly or not at all, you are destined to rent to irresponsible residents who will ultimately cost you on all levels. If it is done inconsistently or improperly, you could open yourself up to fair housing problems. When you screen properly, you will have more responsible residents, fewer problems and a better bottom line.

1. Make sure every step of your screening process is well thought out, complies with fair housing requirements and is in writing.

2. Follow the same procedures for every applicant.

3. Make sure all blanks on the application have been filled in by the applicant, either with information or an "n/a" for "not applicable." Be sure all information is legible. Mistaking an "a" for an "o" could result in a "no record found" in a credit report.

4. Use a screening checklist that notes each source of information used, who you talked to and what was said and when. We suggest you run a credit check; eviction check; rental history verification; bank account confirmation; employment verification, if employed; and check other financial resources if not employed.

Be aware that evictions that do not involve money, such as an eviction for possession of the property only, are not reported on a credit report—only judgments involving money are reported. If you want eviction information that did not result in a money judgment, you need to use a screening company that checks eviction filings at court. However, landlords should take note of AB 2819, effective January 1, 2017, which drastically changed the availability of public eviction records, by sealing all court records in eviction actions unless (1) the plaintiff (landlord) prevails within 60 days of filing or (2) after 60 days only if judgment against all defendants has been entered for the plaintiff after a trial and the court issues an order allowing public access to the record. Absent the above, only persons specifically authorized under the law may request access to the records.

5. Be sure the application provides for signed authorization by the applicant to obtain the applicant's credit report and investigate consumer reports. If you run an eviction search, criminal background check or check landlord references, specific authorization should be obtained.

6. When you compare the application with the information on the credit report, be sure you have the same person. Applicants with something to hide may use a family member's or someone else's information.

7. When contacting a former owner or manager to verify information, do not ask subjective or "opinion" questions (such as "would you rent to this person again?"). Stick to objective information regarding performance of the lease or agreement, such as asking for the dates of tenancy and amount of rent paid, and confirming compliance with the contract by asking questions such as if rent was paid on time, if there were documented, verified complaints from other residents; etc. Many companies prefer to fax a written reference form to the former landlord to gather this information so there will be evidence of what information was exchanged. (*Refer to the list of reference questions in the Appendix for more information.*)

8. If you are contacted by another manager to verify rental history, provide only factual, not subjective, information. If you give *undeserved positive* references just to get rid of the resident, you could be sued for damages incurred by the next landlord based on fraud. Conversely, if you give *undeserved negative* references, you could be sued by the applicant for libel or slander.

9. Do not turn away an applicant because he or she doesn't have a social security number. Ask your credit-reporting agency to run a manual credit report on the person. Refusing to rent to persons without social security numbers could be alleged to have a disparate impact based on national origin for persons from other countries. For example, someone could be a foreign student or come to the U.S. for an extended visit with family members and need an apartment for six months.

   ■ For example, if a Mexican citizen wishes to travel to the U.S. for short-term business or tourism, they must obtain a non-immigrant "tourist" visa from the U.S. Consulate General, but they do not need a U.S. social security number.

10. Attach your screening information to the application. If there was a denial, specify the reason(s). Maintain the records for a minimum of three, preferably four, years.

11. If the applicant found another apartment, was no longer interested or simply changed his mind about your property, note this in his file, including the date of notification and the reason. ◆

Section 8
(Tenant-based Housing Choice Voucher Program)

As of this writing (1/18), Section 8 remains a voluntary program for owners and property management companies in much of the U.S. While Section 8 is a protected classification in a dozen other states, it is not currently protected in California.

However, there is ongoing pressure from advocacy groups and through court cases to require landlords to accept Section 8 vouchers as a source of income. Additionally, several counties and cities have passed local ordinances identifying Section 8 vouchers and other rental assistance programs as protected sources of income.

We anticipate there will continue to be pressure from advocacy groups for additional cities to pass similar laws. (Note that tax credit and some other affordable programs require that the property accept Section 8 vouchers.) There are both benefits and drawbacks to the program, which vary depending on the area of the state you live in and the responsiveness of the administering organization.

If you do not participate in the program and an applicant asks about it, avoid saying, "We don't take Section 8." Instead, we recommend you say, "I'm sorry, but we don't currently participate in the Section 8 program." But you are welcome to apply without the subsidy."

Additionally, avoid referring to the program in your advertisements, such as "No Section 8" or even "Section 8 okay." Both are considered to be negative by fair housing advocates. (Note: if you provide several affordable housing programs at a property, you may be required by those programs to promote their availability. In that case, you might advertise, "Ask about our affordable programs.")

There are also "enhanced Section 8 vouchers" that are given to persons who are displaced from project-based HUD-subsidized housing when the HUD loan ends and the property converts to market rents. Briefly, these enhanced vouchers may exceed the public housing authority's payment standard, allowing payment of any rent that is determined reasonable by the housing authority. They also give the resident the right to remain in the unit after conversion, creating a continuing obligation for the owner to accept the voucher. For information on these vouchers, visit:

http://www.hud.gov/offices/pih/publications/notices/00/pih2000-9.pdf.

If a current resident wants to go on Section 8

If this is a long-term, responsible resident, and you would like to keep the resident, you may want to consider establishing a written policy that says you will accept a Section 8 voucher from any residents in good-standing who have lived on the property for "X" number of years. As representatives of landlords, we would argue that as long as this policy is based on objective business standards, it should not be considered discriminatory as long as it is applied equally to all similarly situated residents going forward. The program's former "take one, take all" policy from many years ago is no longer in effect.

If a current resident or an applicant asks you to accept a Section 8 voucher as an accommodation for disability, the request will need to be evaluated. We recommend that you get legal assistance from a fair housing knowledgeable attorney if you are faced with this situation. ◆

Senior Housing

The issues and requirements involving senior housing are some of the most complex and confusing of all fair housing and landlord-tenant laws. The following is a brief overview.

Except for several federally-subsidized programs for "elderly" housing and senior mobile home parks, senior housing in California falls under the California Unruh Act, which is incorporated into the Fair Employment and Housing Act. Sometimes the federal and state laws contradict each other—often they are extremely unclear. Consequently, it is recommended that you get advice from an attorney who is knowledgeable about this area of housing law for any questions concerning senior housing.

Under the Unruh Act, senior housing falls under two general age requirements:

55 years of age and over

In California, whenever a vacant apartment is re-rented, at least one member of the household must be 55 years of age or older ("qualifying senior") in this category of senior housing.

In most cases, the age requirement for other "qualified permanent residents" in the household is 45. There is an exemption for the spouse or cohabitant or a person who provides primary economic or physical support for the qualifying senior—these people can be any age. The *bona fide* caregiver of a qualifying senior or qualified permanent resident with a disability could also be under 45. There is also an exception for a child or grandchild with a disability who needs to live with the qualifying senior or qualified permanent resident due to the disability. (These are general guidelines; you should seek advice for your specific situation to avoid the loss of your community's senior status.)

62 years of age and over

This category is less complex than the 55+ community and the age requirements are governed by federal law. All residents living on the property must be 62 years of age or older. There are several exceptions.

1. A *bona fide* caregiver would be excepted as a reasonable accommodation based on disability.

2. Another exception is made for employees and their families who are not 62, whose responsibilities require them to live on the property.

Note that the Unruh Civil Rights Act, CC 51, which governs senior housing in California, is provided in the Appendix of this Encyclopedia.

Other requirements and issues

In California (except for Riverside County, which has some exceptions):

- To establish a new 55+ senior property, you must have at least 35 senior units, not counting the manager's unit. (20 units in Riverside.)
- You cannot ask, insist on, or show a preference for, persons who are able to live "independently." A person with a disability who meets your age, rental and financial qualification is entitled to have a caregiver if necessary.

- Newly-constructed senior properties or converted properties must be designed to meet the physical and social needs of seniors. Examples are listed in the Unruh Act, *Civil Code §51*.

- California law does not permit you to rent to underage persons with disabilities in a 55+ senior community without a qualifying senior living in the unit. (In a 62+ property, an underage person with a disability would not be permitted to live there since all residents must be 62 or older.) All units must be rented in accordance with senior housing laws. The only exceptions are several specific project-based HUD "elderly/disabled" subsidized properties, in which case you must follow the HUD regulations requiring you to rent to underage persons with disabilities.

- Don't advertise your property as an "active adult" or "active senior" community. First, there is no such thing as an "adult" community. All housing must be open to persons of all ages (including families with children) except for *bona fide* senior housing[5]. Second, using the word "active" implies that persons with disabilities or who need the assistance of a caregiver are not welcome. Recent cases have held that use of the words "active adult" to advertise senior housing violates fair housing laws. Instead, advertise your community as "Senior 55+" or "Senior 62+" or "55 [or 62] and older."

- Federal law requires that your documentation (advertising, rental criteria, applications, agreements, etc.) must demonstrate intent to operate as senior housing.

---

5. CFR §100.306 (b) states: "Phrases such as 'adult living,' 'adult community,' or similar statements in any written advertisement or prospectus are not consistent with the intent that the housing facility or community intends to operate as housing for persons 55 years of age or older."

- You must have a procedure in place that ensures residents meet your age requirements. Federal law requires that you conduct a survey or use other means to update your resident information every two years to verify that all residents qualify to live in a senior property.

- Most special HUD projects for the elderly and persons with disabilities, as well as public housing, must allow residents to have up to two pets. California law has similar provisions for elderly and disabled persons living in state, county and local public housing.

Issues in senior properties not only involve different laws, they often involve a variety of subsidy programs—too numerous to discuss here. Because of the complexity, we recommend that owners and managers of senior properties seek competent legal guidance when drafting their rental criteria and other leasing documents or when faced with a problem. The risk of failure to comply with applicable rules has serious consequences—such as losing the senior status of the property and, in some cases, potentially losing the subsidy or tax credits. ◆

Sex Offenders

In 1994, the federal government passed "Megan's Law" based on the kidnapping and murder of Megan Kanka, a seven-year-old girl from Hamilton Township, New Jersey. She had been raped and murdered by a twice-convicted sex offender who lived across the street. California also passed a similar Megan's Law *(Penal Code Section 290, et. seq.)* in 1998. Basically, it gives persons the opportunity to find out if a registered sex offender is living in their area so they can use more caution regarding the safety of their children.

Currently, specific information about sex offenders can be found on the California Department of Justice web site at:

http://www.meganslaw.ca.gov

Denying housing to registered sex offenders

Some management companies (especially those who manage property in states other than California) have established policies that exclude registered sex offenders from renting at any of their properties. While exclusion of sex offenders is mandated in project-based HUD-subsidized housing, it poses a legal risk in conventional housing, tax credit and bond properties in California.

Although sex offenders are not a protected class under fair housing law, Californian's Megan's Law specifically addresses the issue of denial of housing to persons on the list.

Current law in California, *Penal Code Section 290.4,* states that it is illegal to use the information from the registered sex offender list to do any of the following:

(2) Except as authorized under paragraph (1) or any other provision of law, use of any information, for purposes relating to any of the following, and that is disclosed pursuant to this section, is prohibited:

(A) Health insurance.

(B) Insurance.

(C) Loans.

(D) Credit.

(E) Employment.

(F) Education, scholarships, or fellowships.

(G) Housing or accommodations.

(H) Benefits, privileges, or services provided by any business establishment.

Penalties for denying housing based on status of the applicant

You may learn of an applicant's sex offender status during the screening process, or the applicant may disclose his or her sex offender status to you. Denying housing in either case can subject the management to stiff fines and penalties. (Note that if you have a question about handling either one of these situations, you may need legal counsel. As with everything else, there are always some exceptions.)

The penalties for denying any of the services listed in the Penal Code based on the sex offender information are stiff. The same code section says that improper use of the information . . .

(e) "shall make the user liable for the actual damages, and any amount that may be determined by a jury or a court sitting without a jury, not exceeding three times the amount of actual damage, and not less than two hundred fifty dollars ($250), and attorney's fees, exemplary damages, or a civil penalty not exceeding twenty-five thousand dollars ($25,000)."

Residents who are registered sex offenders

If it is brought to your attention (usually by a vigilant parent) that an offender is living on the property, you should first contact the police or sheriff's department for more information.

Do not automatically evict the offender because it would be considered "denial of housing or accommodations" to the person. If the person is a high risk or serious offender, the police will normally notify the neighborhood.

If your residents feel it is their duty to harass a recently revealed sex offender in an effort to get the person to move, you may find it necessary to warn them about the state law that went into effect in 1/1/ 2006. Penal Code 290.46 (j)(1) states, *"Any person who uses information disclosed pursuant to this section to commit a misdemeanor shall be subject to, in addition to any other penalty or fine imposed, a fine of not less than ten thousand dollars ($10,000) and not more than fifty thousand dollars ($50,000)"*

The law also states in subsection(k)(4)(B), *"Whenever there is reasonable cause to believe that any person or group of persons is engaged in a pattern or practice of misuse of the information available via the Internet Web site in violation of paragraph (2), the Attorney General, any district attorney, or city attorney or any person aggrieved by the misuse is authorized to bring a civil action in the appropriate court requesting preventive relief, including an application for a permanent or temporary injunction, restraining order, or other order against the person or group of persons responsible for the pattern or practice of misuse."*

Either of these sections could impact residents if they find out an offender is living on the property and proceed to harass the person. These sections are separate from the section regarding a landlord denying housing to an offender.

A word about the list—it isn't perfect. There are people listed in error. There are address errors. People move and fail to re-reregister. There are people listed who may have been caught with an underage girlfriend when they were barely of legal age themselves many years ago. The current list is a lifetime registry, so there are people who haven't repeated a sex offense in 25 years or more. Beginning in 2021, SB 384 (passed in 2017) will creates tiers of Megan's Law registration (10 years, 20 years and life for adult offenders, and 5 years and 10 years for juvenile offenders), with procedures for termination at the end of the mandated minimum registration period. Low-risk offenders may not be listed in the California sex offender list so you may have former offenders living on the property without knowing it. In other words, you should rely on the police information regarding the level of risk involved with the registered offender. The important thing is that you take reasonable steps to ensure the well-being of your other residents while not violating the legal rights of the registered sex offender.

Required language in rental agreements or leases

In California, there is no provision requiring management to notify residents about a specific offender. Instead, the landlord has the duty to include specific wording in the lease or rental agreement, which was modified in 2006. In not less than eight-point type, the following wording should be inserted in your agreements and leases:

"Registered Sex Offenders Notice: Pursuant to Section 290.46 of the Penal Code, information about specified registered sex offenders is made available to the public via an Internet Web site maintained by the Department of Justice at www.meganslaw.ca.gov. Depending on an offender's criminal history, this information will include either the address at which the offender resides or the community of residence and ZIP Code in which he or she resides." ◆

Sexual Harassment

Fair housing laws are tough when sexual harassment occurs in the landlord-tenant relationship. Whenever you have a situation wherein one person has control of the living or working situation of another, you have the potential for harassment. Sexual harassment is considered to be discrimination based on the protected class of sex. These cases are on the rise throughout the U.S. and represent a growing percentage of complaints in California.

Harassment on your property may occur when a resident harasses another resident, when an employee harasses a resident, when one employee harasses another employee, when a resident harasses an employee or when an outside vendor harasses a resident or employee (or vice versa). California law states that it is a violation of the FEHA if an employer does not take action to protect employees when there is harassment by third parties such as residents (customers), vendors or others. All situations are serious and must be addressed by management as soon as they are brought to the attention of management representatives. A victim isn't required to notify the owner before filing a complaint.

One of the most frequent forms of sexual harassment by management occurs in situations involving young, single mothers who can't afford to move. When this type of harassment is uncovered, the perpetrator is often found to have harassed multiple residents over time. (While the perpetrator could be a female, in most cases, it is a male.)

HUD issued Sexual Harassment Guidelines (11/08) that state if management *"knows or should have known that an employee, agent or contractor is sexually harassing applicants, tenants or residents, he or she has the duty to take action to stop the harassment."* The *"owner or manager may be either directly or vicariously liable for sexual harassment . . . committed by employees or agents within the scope of the agency relationship."*

Failure to curb such harassment can be a very costly proposition for a company or owner. For example, in late 2015, a multimillion federal lawsuit was filed by the U.S. Housing and Urban Development Department based on An alleged sex-for-repair scheme. The lawsuit resulted in a $7.9 million settlement to over 100 Baltimore female public housing tenants who were victimized by maintenance workers. The underlying lawsuit alleged that <u>maintenance workers demanded sexual favors in exchange for making repairs</u>. When the women did not comply, repairs were not made thus exposing the tenants to poor living conditions involving mold, pest infestations, lack of heat and risk of electrocution.

Sexual harassment defined

Hostile environment: This occurs when there are deliberate or repeated unsolicited, unwanted, verbal comments about the person's features, or there is physical contact that makes for an offensive environment. It can also include displaying sexual pictures, calendars or emails; leering; stalking or other offensive actions.

Quid pro quo: This occurs when sexual favors are sought as an exchange for housing benefits. For example, telling the resident that you will forget about a late charge or security deposit or you will make the needed repair if she/he will go out with you or grant sexual favors in return.

Best practices suggested by HUD
Currently, HUD suggests the following five practices regarding sexual harassment:

1. Adopt written policies against sexual harassment.
2. Develop a procedure for applicants and residents to report such harassment.
3. Establish sanctions for those who engage in harassment.
4. Educate employees, vendors, residents and applicants about these policies and the Fair Housing Act.
5. Enforce the policies.

Points to remember:

- If a resident complains about harassment by a staff member or another resident, or if staff observes harassment occurring on the property, let the property manager or owner know immediately. The situation must be investigated promptly in accordance with your company's written procedure. Contact an employment attorney to make sure you proceed legally if the accused is an employee. Be sure all employees know that harassment can be grounds for termination. It is advisable to have a written employment agreement that includes such information.

- Managers and maintenance personnel should be careful to avoid behavior that might be construed as discriminatory. Don't tell or e-mail off-color jokes. Beware of making compliments that could sound like come-ons. *It is not what you intend, it is how it is received that counts.*

- If an employee arrives at a resident's apartment prepared to make a requested repair or conduct other business and is met at the door (or at some time during the visit) by an inappropriately attired resident, the employee should excuse him/herself and say he/she will be back at a more convenient time for the resident. Then he/she should promptly inform the manager and document the incident. Reschedule the appointment, and take a witness next time.

- If, during the course of making a repair, a resident makes sexual advances to the maintenance person, the employee should have an escape plan. The situation should be documented, and a witness should accompany the maintenance tech person to finish the repair.

- An employee should never enter a unit without notice to the resident unless there is an emergency. Whenever entering, the prescribed company procedure should be followed. Always knock loudly. No one wants to be caught half undressed or in the shower by management personnel who assumed no one was at home and just let himself in. And the last thing an employee wants is to be accused of sexual harassment.

- We strongly recommend against entering a unit if there are children under the age of 18 present with no adult, even if it is in response to a request for maintenance and the parents give you permission. If there is an emergency, take a witness with you. Children should not be asked to go outside while repairs are made; something could happen to the child.

- Avoid consensual (romantic) relationships between employees and residents. If they go sour, as many relationships do, there can be harassment accusations or other problems. Having such a history can also impact an eviction. If the eviction is for anything other than non-payment of rent, the resident may claim the eviction is in retaliation for the relationship having ended.

- Applicants for employment should be screened carefully. Although California law states that it is a violation of law to deny employment based on a person's presence on the registered sex offender list, it is extremely risky to hire a sex offender as an on-site employee. The person has access to keys to all the apartments, often knows when children or women are alone in their homes, may have access to personal information from the resident's files and is in a position of trust for the residents. (Be sure to seek legal advice from an attorney who specializes in employment law prior to deciding to deny employment based on a person's presence on the sex offender registry.)

- Reminder: if a resident is accused of sexually harassing another resident or an employee, you need to take the complaint seriously and investigate, taking reasonable steps to resolve the matter and documenting every aspect. Be sure you have competent legal advice along the way. ◆

Smoking: Second-& Third-hand Smoke

Second-hand smoke is a common problem for residents and managers alike. In California, recent statistics show that only about 13% of the population smokes, and the rate continues to drop. There are no laws protecting smokers as a protected class, but there are laws regulating where smoking is permitted. In recent years, a number of cities in California have enacted ordinances requiring that multi-unit residential developments prohibit smoking in certain portions of their communities, such as the common areas.[6]

---

6. A current list of cities, and more information about local smoke free laws, is available at: http://center4tobaccopolicy.org/tobacco-policy/smokefree-multi-unit-housing. Be sure you know what smoking laws are in effect or may go into effect wherever your properties are located.

On November 30, 2015, HUD published a new final rule banning smoking in all public housing, which includes prohibiting smoking of tobacco products in all units, indoor common areas, and outdoor common areas within 25 feet of housing and/or administrative offices. At present, the rule only applies to Public Housing Authorities who operate public housing.

California law specifically allows (but doesn't require) a landlord to prohibit smoking in some or all areas of a residential rental property.

There are many reasons for concern about smoking in apartments:

- Smoke damages walls, carpets, window coverings and other surfaces in the apartment and, when concentrated, can be very difficult or impossible to eliminate or cover. Drywall, vents, carpets and window coverings may require replacement.

- Smoldering cigarettes are the leading cause of fire deaths and a common cause of residential fires.

- The U. S. Surgeon General's report (July 2006) found that there are serious health risks posed by second-hand smoke. Such risk can affect other residents of the property, posing, in turn, a risk for the landlord.

- Many residents are highly allergic to tobacco smoke.

- Residents with respiratory diseases who are subjected to others' second-hand smoke must be accommodated in accordance with fair housing law.

The Surgeon General's Report concludes that there are considerable health issues caused by exposure to secondhand smoke and that

> *"5. Eliminating smoking in indoor spaces fully protects nonsmokers from exposure to secondhand smoke. Separating smokers from nonsmokers, cleaning the air, and ventilating buildings cannot eliminate exposures of nonsmokers to secondhand smoke."*

Smoking will become an even greater issue due to Proposition 64, which legalized recreational marijuana in California (*See the subsections on marijuana and medical marijuana smoke below).*

Handling complaints
If you do not have a smoke-free community, when a resident complains about a neighbor's drifting smoke, you should gather more information.

Is the complaining resident physically suffering from the second-hand smoke? Does the complaining resident have a disability that is aggravated by the smoke? This is tricky since you can't ask someone about his or her status in a protected class, but in most cases, the complaining resident will be quick to tell you of his or disability. If the resident indicates that smoke aggravates a disability, you need to accommodate the resident to the best of your ability. Some of these options may provide some relief:

- Try to work something out with the smokers, such as providing smokeless ashtrays or more effective "smoke-eaters."

- To the extent possible, eliminate any entryways for the smoke to seep into the complaining resident's dwelling.

- You may elect to leave the residents to work it out (if no disability is involved), or you may resolve the difficulty by allowing one of the parties to opt out of their lease without penalty.

- One of them may be willing to move. If the smoker is willing to transfer, consider making the vacant unit a "non-smoking" unit for the next resident to try to prevent the person with a disability from being further exposed to second-hand smoke from their new neighbors.

- You may encounter competing disabilities if one resident has respiratory disabilities and the other resident needs medical marijuana for a medical condition. When a situation such as this arises, you are wise to obtain legal advice before taking any further steps.

Treating drifting smoke as a nuisance in your lease
Some of the local ordinances in California allow residents to file a nuisance complaint against another resident based on drifting smoke.

As a potential preventive measure, you can add to your lease the following paragraph regarding noise and other nuisances or disturbances:

> "This includes, but is not limited to, smoking by Resident, household members or guests in such a way as to create a nuisance or disturb the enjoyment of the Apartment Community by other residents (including, but not limited to, neighbors in adjoining units)."

Be aware that a court may be reluctant to evict a resident for smoking—even with the presence of such language in the lease – unless the lease actually prohibits smoking. That said, however, an Orange County jury has found a homeowners association negligent for failing to resolve a secondhand smoke dispute between neighbors at a Trabuco Canyon condominium.

After a five-week trial, Superior Court jurors awarded a family more than $15,000, finding the condo association and management failed to ensure the non-smoking family's right to the "quiet enjoyment" of their own unit.

Third-Hand Smoke

Recent studies have shown that there can also be exposure to "third-hand smoke." Third-hand smoke has been described as "...the nicotine residue that is left behind on furniture, walls, and carpeting after a cigarette has been smoked in a room" that "can become airborne a second time." The particulates are so small that they can penetrate into the deepest parts of the lung, and over time, scientists say, could contribute to breathing problems like asthma or even cancer. The residue also includes heavy metals, carcinogens and even radioactive materials that young children can get on their hands and can ingest, especially when they're crawling or playing on the floor.

A 2011 study, which was conducted on the effects of third-hand smoke in apartments by San Diego State University, tested apartments after smokers moved out and non-smoking families moved in. It found that the compounds were present in some apartments six months to a year later, even though the apartments were cleaned and painted. It also found signs of nicotine in the urine of children.

In 2014 at the American Chemical Society (ACS) Exposition in Dallas, Bo Hang, PH.D., a scientist at Lawrence Berkeley National Laboratory (LBNL), noted that evidence strongly suggests third-hand smoke could threaten human health and that, "The best argument for instituting a ban on smoking indoors is actually third-hand smoke," said Hang.

This is another issue that your company can consider when deciding whether to make communities smoke-free.

Marijuana and medical marijuana smoke

Recreational use of marijuana was legalized in late 2016 by Proposition 64. Under this new state law, codified in California Health and Safety Code §11362 et seq., persons 21 years of age and older are legally allowed to possess, process, transport, purchase, obtain or give away (without compensation) up to 28.5 grams of non-concentrated cannabis and up to 8 grams of concentrated cannabis and possess, plant, cultivate, harvest, dry or process up to 6 living plants. Under the law, cannabis (including the living plants), may be stored within a person's private residence, or on the private grounds of a private residence, in a locked space which is not visible from a public place by normal unaided vision.

Private residences include single family residences as well as multi-family properties. Additional limitations apply as specified within the law.

While the impact this new law will have on landlords and residential properties remains to be seen, we can anticipate a likely rise of marijuana use at residential properties statewide. Landlords may choose to prohibit marijuana smoking and cultivation. However, landlords who choose to prohibit marijuana smoking and cultivation should expect to continue to encounter issues with residents claiming they need to smoke or cultivate marijuana for medical purposes, which raises issues relative to disability-related accommodations. Proposition 64 did not change California's medical marijuana laws.

Use, cultivation and possession of marijuana for medical use have been "decriminalized" in California under the Compassionate Use Act (CUA) and the Medical Marijuana Program (MMP), which implements and clarifies the CUA. Many residents and some fair housing advocacy groups argue that allowing the use of medical marijuana in residential rental housing is a reasonable accommodation for disability.

Although both recreational and medical marijuana can be used under California law, marijuana possession, use and sale (for **any** reason) is still a violation of federal law.

Some landlords prohibit marijuana use or growth, even for medical purposes based on it being illegal under federal law. Note that HUD's position with regard to public housing and privately owned/operated, project-based HUD-subsidized housing is that a person who admits to using marijuana for medical reasons must be denied admission to the housing. With regard to current residents who are using medical marijuana, HUD mandates that operators of such properties develop a written policy, which can include eviction from the project.

Other landlords treat medical marijuana as a disability accommodation issue and focus on the "reasonableness" of the resident's actions. If medical marijuana use is creating a nuisance for other residents, the landlord has a responsibility to address the issue by demanding the user stop creating a nuisance. You may have to explore other ways to accommodate that don't create a nuisance.

More recently, many more persons who need the benefits of medical marijuana are using medical cannabis oil, which, when prescribed for particular illnesses, can be more effective than smoking or ingesting marijuana.

When the oils are used, you are less likely to have other residents be concerned about the drifting smoke and, in fact likely won't even know it is being used.

Meanwhile, get legal advice if faced with a medical marijuana situation on your property.

Non-smoking properties

Since California law clearly allows landlords to prohibit smoking on the property, you may designate your entire community as a non-smoking property, or any portion therein, such as a non-smoking building, floor or group of units or smoke-free common areas. Focus on "non-smoking" or "smoke-free) rather than "smokers," considering the behavior or action, not the person.

In order to make a successful conversion to a smoke-free property, you should develop a plan that will cause the least amount of disruption—such as grandfathering in existing smokers but making a unit non-smoking once the smoking resident moves out. KTS attorneys can help you with the legal steps to take in order to make the transition. There are also a number of websites that can provide management with the necessary tools to make the transition work.

Note that in privately owned/operated HUD subsidized properties, while HUD encourages the reduction of smoking with regard to new residents, they do not allow eviction of subsidized housing recipients who resided on the property when the rules were changed.

Although you may slightly limit your potential resident pool with a non-smoking property, you may attract more non-smoking residents who prefer or need to avoid second-hand smoke. You will eliminate the complaints and liabilities of drifting smoke, reduce fire risks and eliminate the costs of smoke damage. Ultimately, it's your choice.

Electronic Cigarettes:

E-cigarettes have become a popular method of delivering nicotine for many people, including children who are attracted to their various flavors. They are currently unregulated in the U.S. but emerging research indicates that there are a number of health risks associated with them. They have been banned in some countries, such as Australia, Canada, Israel and Mexico, while other countries are in the process of regulating them.

In the meantime, there are several considerations for management: Advertised as smoke-free, e-cigarettes may be a solution for drifting secondhand smoke issues unless the secondhand vapor also creates health issues for neighbors.

- If you have a smoke-free property, will you allow e-cigarettes?

- Will you allow medical marijuana to be smoked in e-cigarettes?

- Many California cities have passed ordinances prohibiting the use of e-cigarettes where smoking is prohibited. ◆

"Steering"

Steering is a discriminatory act that occurs when owners or managers direct applicants to certain locations on the property *because* they are from a protected class. Or they may say things that would discourage an applicant from living on their property. Steering is generally defined as attempting to control the outcome of where a person lives based on his or her protected class. Some examples include:

- Encouraging families with children to live

   a) near the playground,

   b) in a downstairs unit,

   c) in an end unit,

   d) in a unit over a garage,

   e) in a particular building,

   f) in a particular section of the community, or

   g) in another apartment community down the street or across town.

- Encouraging applicants with disabilities to select a downstairs unit.

- Suggesting to persons of color or a certain nationality that they should live in a particular section of the community or building or another part of town.

- Situating the elderly or persons with disabilities in a particular building or section of the community.

- Directing persons from a protected class to undesirable units, such as an unprepared unit, the most distant one or one that overlooks the dumpster area, in hopes that they won't want to live there.

If an applicant volunteers that he or she wants a downstairs unit or one by the playground, that's fine. (Document the fact that they made the request.) It only becomes steering when you subtly encourage it or suggest it first. The best policy is to let applicants know what you have available, then let them decide which dwelling they want. Remember, everyone is entitled to equal housing opportunities.

Other potential "steering" situations
If an applicant says he or she would like to live next to "someone like myself" or someone who is the "same nationality" or who "has children" or "doesn't have any children," let the applicant know you cannot accommodate their request. Remind them that you are an equal opportunity housing provider and all units are open to all qualified people. If necessary, explain that you do not keep such records on your residents and cannot discuss such issues because of fair housing laws. ◆

Subsidized v. Conventional Housing

There are a number of differences that have fair housing implications between government-subsidized housing and conventional housing (which receives no subsidies). The types of housing we are referring to as "subsidized" are *project-based HUD properties*, meaning that the property or portions of the property have certain federal loans, grants, mortgages, loan and mortgage insurance or other federal assistance. It does not include properties that accept Section 8 vouchers (which is a *tenant-based* subsidy) and have no other government funding. Nor does it include bond properties (or other similar affordable programs) that have no project-based HUD-subsidized components. Tax credit properties are sometimes required to follow some of the same rules as HUD properties.

Some examples of the differences include the following:

▪ **Asking for demographic information of residents**
Subsidized and tax credit properties are usually required by their respective programs to gather information about residents, such as race, sex, familial status, etc. The purpose is to ensure that the beneficiaries of the subsidy are diverse. However, it would be a fair housing violation for a conventional property to gather information regarding protected classes before or during tenancy.

- **Promotions/advertising**

Subsidized properties are required to have a written Affirmative Fair Housing Advertising Plan that meets HUD requirements, showing how the property will be reaching out to persons who could qualify for the property. Conventional housing is not required to have such a plan, but it is still a good idea to have a plan that reaches out to those who wouldn't necessary know about the housing opportunities you have available (affirmative marketing).

- **Occupancy standards**

HUD occupancy guidelines for conventional housing can differ from those established by DFEH in California. HUD indicates that restricting occupancy to 2 persons per bedroom does not usually discriminate against families, while DFEH suggests allowing at least 2 persons per bedroom plus one in the unit.

Some subsidized programs have minimum limitations. For example, to maximize the use of affordable units and maximize the use of government tax dollars, one person may be restricted to a smaller unit rather than allowing one person to rent a three-bedroom apartment that would be better suited to a larger family's needs. If there is a federal program directive that requires such guidelines in order to establish program eligibility, a housing provider may be successful in using that directive as a defense in a discrimination case based on state law violations.

In conventional housing, owners are wise to adhere to the occupancy standard guidelines used by DFEH (not setting a minimum but setting a maximum that is not less than two persons per bedroom plus one additional person for the unit) unless the property is located in a city, such as San Francisco, where local law dictates broader occupancy standards.

- **Qualifying**

Persons who want to rent in a subsidized property have to meet two types of requirements. First, they have to be *eligible for the program* (such as family income limits, and provision of social security numbers for all family members over age 6, with some allowances). Second, they have to be *eligible for the property*. In both subsidized and conventional housing, the owner is allowed to establish reasonable, non-discriminatory rental criteria.

Subsidized properties are required to have in place a Tenant Selection Plan that meets the HUD requirements and covers both the program and property qualifications.

- **Application fees**

There are no application fees in subsidized housing. The property pays for all screening costs. In conventional housing, an application fee may be charged in accordance with California Civil Code 1950.6.

- **Re-qualifying**

All residents in subsidized properties must be "recertified" every year to make sure they still qualify for the size unit they occupy and continue to meet the program limitations. There is no good business reason to requalify every resident in conventional housing unless the resident is transferring to a more expensive apartment and must prove that they will meet the income requirements for that unit.

- **Disability**

Subsidized properties and properties that receive other federal funding (such as HOME, CBDG, etc.) are required to have units that are specifically designed for persons with physical disabilities (wheelchair accessible) and for persons with hearing or vision impairments. Consequently, the rental applications for such properties will ask if the person or a household member qualifies for one of these units. Conventional properties should not ask for this information.

If a resident with a disability needs a reasonable modification to his or her unit in a subsidized property or a property that receives other federal funding (such as HOME, CBDG, etc.), the property pays for it unless it is so costly that it would cause an ***undue*** financial burden to the property. In that case, the property has the option of paying for what it can afford with the resident paying for the remainder of the cost. In conventional property, the resident pays for the reasonable modification.

Subsidized and other federally-funded properties must also adhere to all the requirements of Section 504 of the Rehabilitation Act of 1973. This law focuses on disability accommodations in all government-subsidized programs, including housing, such as requiring 5% of the total units to be physically accessible and 2% to be hearing and visually accessible. Those units must be distributed throughout the property (i.e., they cannot be all located in one particular area of the property).

A compliance staff member should be assigned the responsibility of ensuring that all 504 requirements are met.

- **Senior housing**

If a subsidized property operates under a project-based "elderly/disabled" HUD program, such as 202 Supportive Housing for the Elderly, the property may be required to accept persons with disabilities who do not meet the age

In contrast, California law requires senior communities to strictly follow the state's age guidelines or risk losing their senior status.

However, California law was amended to provide that selection preferences based on age, imposed in connection with federally-approved housing programs, do not constitute age discrimination in housing. Accordingly, a California housing provider participating in a HUD elderly or elderly/disabled program can now rest assured that following the HUD program requirements will not subject them to liability for discrimination based on a violation of California's senior housing laws.

- **Megan's Law**

Project-based HUD-subsidized housing programs do not allow registered sex offenders to live on the property. However, in California, you cannot deny housing in conventional properties if the information comes from the registry's web site. To do otherwise could subject the owner to potential fines of up to $25,000 and other penalties. ◆

Testing

The mere thought of "testing" or having a "tester" visit a property brings chills to most owners and managers. Many believe they could be "set up" for a fair housing violation—much like a sting operation. However, testing used as part of the investigation of a complaint is nothing like that. While it can show that there may be discrimination occurring, it can also show that there is NO evidence of discrimination.

Types of testing
Compliance Testing:
In most cases, testing is carried out in response to a fair housing complaint, usually involving the leasing process. *Bona fide* testers are seldom asked to randomly try to catch managers doing something wrong.
Audits or Surveys:
Audits are usually performed at the request of a local municipality, although HUD and the Department of Justice or local fair housing organizations occasionally conduct them. They are designed to determine the current level of discrimination in a given area for a specific protected class. The information is generally used for statistical analysis but could be used for enforcement purposes.

Systemic discrimination testing

Because discrimination rarely occurs openly these days, private and governmental enforcement organizations throughout the country are routinely conducting "systemic" testing in which policies or practices that result in discriminatory effect or disparate impact can be uncovered. If violations are brought to light, chances are good that complaints may be filed. These agencies have received additional federal funding in recent years to conduct this type of testing so it is becoming more common.

Becoming a tester

Testers are recruited by the testing agency (almost always a local fair housing organization) from a variety of sources, such as community colleges. A tester must be sharp, unbiased, able to successfully assume specific characteristics and capable of testifying in court when necessary. A candidate who has a grudge against managers and owners can't become a tester because the test could be biased and therefore worthless. The test must be accurate and fair because it must be able to stand up to scrutiny in court, if necessary. On the flip side, apartment managers wouldn't be selected as testers because they would be testing their competitors, which would be a conflict of interest. However, they might be acceptable testers for lending or insurance testing.

Testers are screened and well-trained by the agency. They are paid a stipend for their services, which is minimal considering the time involved in performing the test, completing the report and debriefing.

The testing process

Let's say a complaint based on race has been filed. The agency would ordinarily send out two testers, one Caucasian and one of the complainant's race. This is called paired testing. Testers are not told the nature of the complaint. They are not permitted to discuss anything of a discriminatory nature or to be drawn into such a discussion with the manager or leasing agent. Each tester completes a neutral report and is debriefed to make sure all information is complete, accurate and readable. The reports are then compared to see if there are differences in the way the two testers were treated. The results then become part of the case—providing either evidence that supports potential discrimination or showing that there is no testing evidence to support it. In many tests, the tester won't realize he or she has been discriminated against. It may not be apparent until the two test reports are compared.

Testers have the right to sue
While a rare occurrence, testers have "standing," or the right to sue, in a fair housing case. It is important to keep in mind that it can be just as painful an experience for a tester to realize he or she has been discriminated against as an actual applicant. No one likes to be rejected or treated badly because of how they look or where their parents came from. ◆

Vendors

The companies that supply rental properties with goods and services have the opportunity and potential to discriminate against residents, guests or staff. Because they have been invited to work on the property, they are deemed agents of the owner and management. If a vendor does something illegal, the vendor, property owner and management company may share the legal responsibility. In 2016, HUD updated the Code of Federal Regulations to clarify who may be liable for discriminatory housing practices. HUD defines two types of liability: direct liability and vicarious liability. Under CFR §100.7, states:

(a) *Direct liability. (1) A person is directly liable for: (i) the person's own conduct that results in a discriminatory housing practice. (ii) Failing to take prompt action to correct and end a discriminatory housing practice by that person's employee or agent, where the person knew or should have known of the discriminatory conduct. (iii) Failing to take prompt action to correct and end a discriminatory housing practice by a third-party, where the person knew or should have known of the discriminatory conduct and had the power to correct it.*

(b) *Vicarious liability. A person is vicariously liable for a discriminatory housing practice by the person's agent or employee, regardless of whether the person knew or should have known of the conduct that resulted in a discriminatory housing practice, consistent with agency law.*

It is therefore important that all vendor personnel understand fair housing rules and work with management to reduce the risk of discriminatory acts occurring. More and more management companies require vendors to sign an agreement stating that none of the vendor's personnel will discriminate against any residents.

- It is inappropriate for a vendor or a vendor's employee to make any overly friendly advances or comments to any resident, guest or staff member. Whether or not there was intent to harass, anything that could be construed as sexual harassment by the resident could be the basis for a claim against the landlord.

- Vendors shouldn't make belittling comments about anyone based on their protected class status when on-site. It can be grounds for a complaint.

On the reverse side of the coin:

- Residents do not have the right to treat vendors in a discriminatory manner based on the vendor's status as a member of a protected class. For example, acting rudely or calling service personnel derogatory names based on their national origin or race would be a discriminatory act.

- Management employees should never treat vendors in such a manner.

If any of these situations are brought to the attention of the owner or management, it is incumbent upon management to investigate and take appropriate action if, in fact, discriminatory activities are found to have occurred. This may include contacting the vendor company, reporting the incident and seeking assurances that the vendor company will take appropriate action. If an appropriate resolution is not reached, terminating the contract with the vendor may be in order. ◆

Words and Phrases to Watch For

One of the most common questions asked by managers, leasing professionals and owners in fair housing trainings is, "What can I or can't I say so I won't get in trouble with fair housing?" Although the answer is simple, "don't say or ask anything that could be construed as discriminatory," an appropriate answer requires housing providers to be familiar with the laws and to THINK before they speak. The list of comments that follows can be used to stimulate your thinking and to reevaluate comments that you or your staff might be making:

Referring to a person's protected class

- Is your husband coming with you to see the apartment? (Marital status)

- Do I hear children in the background? How old are they? (Familial status)
- Are our apartments close to where you work? (Source of income)
- I can see how hard it is for you to get around. Do you think you can live independently? (Disability)
- Do you attend church? There's one a block away. (Religion)
- I can't quite tell where you are from by your accent. Where are you from? (National origin)

Chilling or discouraging comments

- I'm worried you might fall, going up and down the stairs by yourself. (Disability)
- Our residents are mostly professionals. (Source of Income)
- This isn't a very safe neighborhood for children, and the schools aren't particularly good in this area either. (Familial status)
- This property isn't very safe for children because: balconies, creek, gangs, fountain, busy street, cliff, stairs, etc. (Familial status)
- We don't have a playground and there's no place for children to play here. (Familial status)

Steering comments

- This property wasn't designed for children. But Acme Apartments down the street has a great playground. (Familial status)
- We prefer to have our families with children live in ground floor units or near the playground. (Familial status)
- You know, I think you'd be much safer living in one of our downstairs apartments. (Disability)
- Most of our seniors like you prefer to live near each other so it's quieter. Would you like to see one of our vacancies in our senior section? (Age)

Indications of other discriminatory practices

- Sorry, but our units are not accessible, so we can't rent to you. (Disability)
- We'll have to charge you a higher security deposit because of your guide dog (or because your wheelchair might damage the door frames). (Disability)

- Sorry, we don't rent to anyone on welfare. (Source of income)
- We can't rent to you and your guide dog because we have a "no pet" policy here. (Disability)
- We only have a few accessible units, and they're full. We can put you on our waiting list for them. (Disability)

When applicants ask discriminatory questions

Applicants unknowingly ask discriminatory questions of housing providers. There can be a fine line between what information is acceptable to provide and what might be discriminatory. When asked by a prospective resident, *"What kind of people live here?"* or a similar inquiry about the make-up of the resident population, respond with, *"We are an equal opportunity housing provider, and anyone who meets our eligibility standards is welcome to live here."* If pushed further, say, *"I'm sorry, but responding to that kind of question is a violation of fair housing law."*

Other common loaded questions from prospects are "Who lives next door?" to the vacant unit or they may request to live in a unit that is "not next to" someone from a certain protected class. With the first question, rather than responding, "Oh, a nice Hispanic family with a new baby" or with a similarly direct answer, you should simply point out that it is occupied by people who have met the property's qualifications at the time they applied. Besides, whoever is living there today may move tomorrow, so you can never really guarantee who someone's neighbors might be.

Other words to avoid

This partial list provides some of the words that should not be used: singles, couples, exclusive, executive, adult, married, infants only, Catholic (or any religious references), employed, welfare, no Section 8, no playground, Hispanic (or any national origin references), mature persons, empty nesters, students, restricted, integrated, traditional, family-oriented or private community. Note that the word *"quiet"* indicates to most families with children that they are not welcome.

Why can't I say that?

If you don't understand why some of these comments are discriminatory or the fair housing laws that apply to them, it's time to give your fair housing IQ an educational boost—or you may find yourself on the receiving end of a complaint. ◆

Glossary of Terms

Blockbusting
The illegal practice of inducing homeowners to sell their properties by making representations regarding the entry or prospective entry of persons of a particular race or national origin into the neighborhood.

Chilling
A form of "steering," it is establishing rules or making comments designed to discourage applicants from renting.

DFEH
(California Department of Fair Employment and Housing) The state administrative agency charged with enforcement of fair housing laws.

Differential Treatment or Disparate Treatment
When practices, policies and services are applied differently to members of different protected classes.

Disparate Impact
A seemingly neutral policy or practice that has a discriminatory effect on one or more protected classes.

DOJ
(U.S. Department of Justice) The Attorney General's office, which handles federal pattern or practice fair housing complaints.

HUD
(U.S. Department of Housing and Urban Development) The federal administrative agency charged with enforcement of fair housing laws.

Otherwise Qualified
The applicant meets your financial, credit and rental history requirements.

Redlining
Illegal practice of discriminating based on geographic location when providing loans or insurance coverage.

Statute of Limitations
The amount of time within which a lawsuit must be filed after an alleged discriminatory action or statement.

Steering
Trying to control the outcome of where someone lives because of his or her protected class.

Neutral Holiday Decorations

There are many ways to decorate for the holidays that celebrate the season rather than a particular religion. Here are some ideas to help you prepare for the exciting and festive days ahead.

Artificial or real fruit

Baskets of fruit

Beaded fruit

Bows

Candles (without religious décor)

Candy canes

Frosty the Snowman

Garlands

Gifts/packages

Gingerbread houses

Gingerbread cookies

Glass balls

Glitter

Greenery

Holly

Icicles

Items painted gold or silver

Mistletoe

Neutral color schemes

Non-religious cookies

Pine cones

Plain lights

Poinsettias

Red and green items

Reindeer

Silk flowers with glitter

Sleds

Snow on windows

Snow

Snowflakes

Snowmen

Strung beads

Strung cranberries and popcorn

Teddy bears in holiday décor

Tinsel

Trees

Wreaths

Court Decision: Reasonable Accommodations for Persons with Disabilities

A decision handed down by the US Court of Appeals for the 9th Circuit has important fair housing implications for residential rental owners and property managers *(Giebeler v. M & B Associates, September 15, 2003)*. <u>Essentially, the decision states that the company discriminated against a person with a disability by not permitting a reasonable accommodation of a co-signer or other reasonable alternative as an exception to the company's "no co-signers" policy.</u>

In this case, the applicant had a good rental history with excellent credit and a good job. When he became ill with AIDS, he could no longer afford his apartment and needed assistance. He found a more affordable apartment that was closer to his mother. Because he didn't meet the community's minimum income requirements of three times the rent at Branham, he was denied residency. His mother went to the manager the next day offering to pay for the apartment on her son's behalf. She had good credit and owned her home outright, and her income met the requirement. This arrangement was rejected by management based on their policy against allowing co-signers on lease agreements. The rental and credit history of the parties were never reviewed by management.

The complaint claimed disparate impact (having a neutral policy that impacts one or more protected classes), intentional discrimination and failure to reasonably accommodate the applicant's disability through refusal to waive the "no co-signers" policy.

The court found that the applicant was not asking for a discounted rent, only a different way of proving that the same rent would be paid for the apartment as anyone else would pay—only that the income relied upon be his mother's instead of his own. The court determined the request was reasonable and necessary in order to fulfill the goals of the Fair Housing Amendments Act of 1988. Ordinarily, an accommodation is reasonable under the FHAA when it imposes no fundamental alteration in the nature of the program or undue financial or administrative burdens.

We continue to include this landmark case in our Encyclopedia because of its continuing importance in cases involving financial accommodations.

Complying with HUD Guidance on Criminal Background Checks

Lynn Dover, Esq.
May, 2016

As most of you are aware, HUD recently released guidance for <u>all</u> housing providers regarding how the use of criminal background checks could potentially violate fair housing laws.

The guidance outlines how using criminal background screening to deny housing can create a disparate impact (discriminatory effect) based on race due to the higher incarceration rates among Hispanics and African Americans relative to their percentage of the total population and when compared against the incarceration rates of non-Hispanic Caucasians. The guidance also outlines HUD's position regarding what is necessary for a housing provider to successfully defend such a complaint.

Unfortunately, the guidance has raised more questions than answers on how to comply. This article will attempt to provide some practical suggestions for eliminating or reducing potential fair housing liability.

1. <u>Deny for Convictions for the Manufacture or Distribution of Controlled Substances</u>:
   This is currently the only way you can be certain your criminal background policies will not lead to fair housing liability. This is because the Fair Housing Act specifically states that landlords do not have to make housing available to persons with such a conviction.[7] The guidance confirms that this remains a "safe harbor." However, it cautions that the exclusion is only for manufacture or distribution (making or selling) controlled substances and does not extend to other drug-related crimes such as use or possession.

---

7. Note that project-based HUD subsidized properties must also prohibit admission to sex offenders subject to a lifetime registration requirement under a state government's sex offender registration program or to individuals found to have manufactured or produced methamphetamine on the premises of federally assisted housing.

---

2. Narrowly Tailor Criminal Background Policies:
   If you want to deny housing based on past convictions for other than the manufacture or distribution of controlled substances, the guidance states that policies must be narrowly tailored and that a landlord must be able to show that its "tailored" use of criminal background checks *"accurately distinguishes between criminal conduct that indicates a demonstrable risk to resident safety and/or property and criminal conduct that does not."* This is going to be a difficult burden to meet. Below are some practical tips for consideration:

   a) No Denial Based on Arrest Records: HUD states that landlords should not use arrest records as a basis for excluding applicants. HUD's reasoning is that an arrest which does not lead to a subsequent conviction does not prove that an individual engaged in illegal activity. Therefore, the use of arrest records would not provide information regarding whether the applicant who was arrested would be a threat to the safety of other residents or their property.

   b) Avoid Blanket Prohibitions: HUD indicates that blanket prohibitions, such as denial of housing to persons with any conviction (or any felony) will not stand up to fair housing scrutiny.

   c) Consider Credit and Other Qualifying Criteria before Criminal History: HUD suggests that housing providers establish a policy under which other qualifying criteria are considered first. For example, you could check the applicant's credit, income, rental history and ability to meet any other qualifying criteria and if the applicant does not qualify, deny the application on that basis. By doing this, you would be able to prove that criminal history did not influence the decision to deny the application and thus no disparate impact discrimination occurred. Criminal history would only be considered if the applicant met all of the other qualifying criteria. While this would not completely eliminate potential liability, it could have the effect of reducing the pool of potential complainants.

   d) Tailor Screening Policies to Focus on Protecting Resident Safety and/or Property: While HUD does not provide specifics on how a housing provider might tailor its policies in this manner, it does provide some general guidelines. It states that criminal screening standards must take into account the "nature and severity" of an individual's conviction, how long ago the criminal activity occurred, and conduct an "individualized assessment" of each applicant, considering "relevant mitigating information" such as: (1) the facts or circumstances surrounding the criminal conduct; (2) the age of the individual at the time the conduct occurred; (3) evidence that the individual has maintained a good tenant history before and after the conviction or conduct; (4) and evidence of rehabilitation efforts. It is recommended that you consider eliminating policies that deny for less serious convictions such as infractions and misdemeanors and focus only on felonies that they reasonably believe would pose a risk to resident safety and/or property. You would then need to decide the length of time since conviction that could be defensible as posing a current threat to resident safety and/or property. Lastly, you would need to conduct the aforementioned individualized assessment for each applicant.

e) Compile Evidence that the Criminal Screening Policies Actually Achieve the Purpose of Protecting Resident Safety and/or Property: HUD gives no insight or examples of how you might prove that your policies actually have the desired effect. Presumably, if you could provide evidence that a property was experiencing high incidents of, and/or police calls to service for, certain prior crimes to implementing the criminal screening standards and that those incidences dropped significantly after the criminal screening was implemented, the burden could be met. This would likely require an individualized assessment on each property.

It is strongly recommended that decisions regarding the policies and individualized assessments be made by owners or upper management rather than by on-site employees and that the policies be reviewed by an attorney with expertise in fair housing before implementation.

Kimball, Tirey & St. John LLP now has a California Application to Lease available for purchase. Our application was developed by our Fair Housing Practice Group to help eliminate potential fair housing risks. It also complies with the new HUD guidance on criminal background screening. Please feel free to contact us at KTSFairHousing@kts-law.com for more information.

Suggestions:

Rental History Verification

Applicant Name _____ Date/Time _____

Circle one: Current Landlord   Previous Landlord

Property Name _____

Address _____

Contact Name _____ Position _____

Phone _____ Fax _____

- When did applicant move in and move out?

- What was the monthly rental amount?

- How many times did applicant pay rent late?

- How many returned NSF checks?

- Was applicant served any notices for non-payment of rent? (If so, how many, when?)

- Was applicant served any notices for lease/rules violations? (If so, what type, how many, when?)

- Did applicant have a pet? (If so, please describe.)

- Did you receive any complaints from other residents about the applicant? (If so, what type, how many and when? In writing? Were they verified?)

- Have you documented any interference or harassment of management by the applicant during the tenancy? (If so, what, how often and when?)

- Did other residents say they were moving out because of problems with this resident? Were the problems verified? What were they?

- Did the applicant damage the property in any way during the tenancy? If so, how? Were the costs of repairing the damage recovered from the applicant?

- Did applicant leave the property in good repair?

- Does applicant owe you any money? (Amount? Judgment/Non-Judgment?)

- Was applicant evicted or asked to leave for cause? (If so, what was the cause?)

(Avoid asking, "Would you rent to this person again?")

Notes:

Web Resources

This list contains some of our favorite Web resources that will help you learn more about fair housing and stay up on some of the new developments.

Government Agencies

- ❑ **HUD** (Housing & Urban Development) *Federal Fair Housing Law and Administrative Law Judge decisions*

    www.hud.gov

- ❑ **DOJ** (Dept. of Justice/Attorney General) *U.S. decisions, ADA*

    www.usdoj.gov

- ❑ **Fair Housing Accessibility First** *Federal design and new construction requirements*
    www.fairhousingfirst.org

- ❑ **DFEH** (California Department of Employment and Housing) *Decisions, timely California fair housing information*

    www.dfeh.ca.gov

- ❑ **CAA** (California Apartment Association) *Wide variety of current California information, plus pending legislation and alerts*

    www.caanet.org

- ❑ **NAA** (National Apartment Association) *Wide variety of current federal information, including pending legislation and alerts*

    www.naahq.org

- ❑ **NMHC** (National Multi Housing Council) *Federal legislative information*
    www.nmhc.org

Other sources of information

- **Kimball, Tirey & St. John LLP** *Fair housing, landlord-tenant and real estate law information, forms, training materials, on-line courses, webinars, publications, consultation, fair housing defense and document reviews*

  Phone: 800-338-6039

  www.kts-law.com

- **California Statutes** *Fair housing laws, landlord-tenant laws, as well as all pending legislation*

  www.leginfo.ca.gov

- **Federal Statutes** *Fair housing, credit reporting, other laws*

  uscode.house.gov/

- **Code of Federal Regulations**

  www.gpoaccess.gov/cfr/index.html

- **National Fair Housing Advocate** *Daily updates on discrimination issues around the country, case database and wide variety of fair housing information. Also federal fair housing laws.*

  www.fairhousing.com

# # #

KTS Fair Housing Resources

At *Kimball, Tirey & St. John LLP, we* recognize the value of preventing problems before they develop. Besides this Fair Housing Encyclopedia, we also offer *other resources to assist our clients with their residential rental housing.*

Educational Opportunities

We train thousands of owners and managers every year through live trainings for clients, apartment associations and other organizations.

Now, it's easier than ever. You can train your management team and still keep the office open by training online.

Online Training

Anyone can register for one of our online trainings through our KTS website. We also partner *with many companies to train their new hires online in "Fair Housing Fundamentals" and "Fair Housing for Maintenance Personnel in English and in Spanish."* These three courses also serve as great, annual refreshers for seasoned personnel to keep them up on current fair housing issues. In addition, we also offer *"Disability Only"* and *"Hoarding,"* which are more in-depth courses for management personnel.

Live Webinars

Our live Webinars are offered periodically and cover topics of greatest and most current interest to clients from fair housing to employment law to landlord/tenant issues.

Webinar Recordings

These one-hour Webinar Recordings include some of our most popular past live Webinars such as hoarding, rules for children, assistive animals, secondhand smoke, legal updates and other important legal topics.

Fair Housing Forms and Opinion Letters

If you are interested in KTS legal trainings, please contact

Education@kts-law.com or 800-338-6039

To access an online training or find an upcoming webinar or past web recording, please visit our Education pageon our website at www.kts-law.com.

Kimball, Tirey & St. John LLP offers its clients a variety of fair housing forms and opinion letters based on legal issues that are common to fair housing situations. Their purpose is to help you make risk management decisions on difficult and confusing issues you face in your operations. Each opinion letter is available for a fee and is customized to the owner, manager or other person requesting the opinion.

Disability Forms Package

We have a forms package for disability situations. The package contains approximately 10 forms covering rules of conduct for assistive animals, verification of disability and need for an accommodation/modification, modification and accommodation request, procedures for handling requests, approval/denial of requests, and a Disability Booklet for both conventional and subsidized housing. Forms are not sold separately.

Other Disability Forms

Also available for purchase are number of individually packaged products addressing several commonly recurring disability situations:

- Caregivers: Includes three types of caregiver agreements (depending on property type)
- Motorized scooter agreements
- Oxygen use & smoking

KTS Residential Rental Application

Rental applications sometimes ask questions or require information that can be problematic from a fair housing perspective and lead to potential fair housing liability. We have developed a Residential Rental Application that is designed to be compliant with federal and state fair housing laws. The Application is available for purchase by contacting the Fair Housing Practice Group at: KTSFairHousing@kts-law.com or (800) 336-6039.

Fair Housing Opinion letters on the following subjects:

- **Companion Animals**
- **Criminal Backgrounds** *(Conventional or Subsidized Housing)*
- **Insurance and Assistive Animals**
- **Medical Marijuana**
- **Megan's Law**
- **Disability-Related Common Area Modifications**
- **Use of Social Security Cards**
- **Smoking and Second-Hand Smoke**

If you are interested in any of these fair housing materials, please contact

Fair Housing at KTSFairHousing@kts-law.com or (800) 338-6039

...for more information and a fee quote.

Other Important Legal Resources

Lease Reviews

Annual lease reviews are an important part of the risk management programs of landlords and property managers. Kimball, Tirey & St. John LLP can provide lease reviews for a reasonable charge. To request a *landlord/tenant review*, contact Jamie Sternberg at Jamie.Sternberg@kts-law.com or (619) 744-0863. For a *fair housing review*, contact our fair housing practice group at: KTSFairHousing@kts-law.com or 800-338-6039.

Live Preventive Law Classes

Kimball, Tirey & St. John LLP offers private classes on various legal subjects geared to meet the needs of residential owners and managers that can be provided at your designated location. These courses will help you comply with today's complex landlord-tenant, fair housing and other laws. We also provide annual public legal seminars: the schedule is available online at http://www.kts-law.com/education/seminars/ or by contacting Client Education at Education@kts-law.com or (800) 338-6039.

Website Information

We have a huge library of articles that are useful to property owners and managers that can be found at our website at http://www.kts-law.com/resources/ .

Books and Publications

Kimball, Tirey & St. John offers several helpful fair housing publications, including

- *The California Fair Housing Encyclopedia*

- The combined *(English and Spanish) Fair Housing Guide for Maintenance and Support Personnel*

- *Establishing Your Rental Criteria Workbook*

These materials, and additional copies of this Fair Housing Encyclopedia, can be ordered online at www.kts-law.com or by contacting Client Education at Education@kts-law.com or (800) 338-6039.

Email Alert System

Get personalized, current legal information to help you operate your business more effectively and in compliance with the law by joining our e-mail alert system. Clients who wish to receive alerts should send us an email at info@kts-law.com. This service is offered without charge to Kimball, Tirey & St. John's clients. ◆